Northern Ireland

50 Years of Self - Government

NORTHERN IRELAND

50 Years of Self-Government

MARTIN WALLACE

DAVID & CHARLES : NEWTON ABBOT

ISBN 0 7153 5252 0

To my Mother and Father

Set in Intertype Cornell
and printed in Great Britain
by Bristol Typesetting Company Limited
for David & Charles (Publishers) Limited
South Devon House   Newton Abbot   Devon

Contents

Preface

There are several reasons at this time for writing an account of the Northern Ireland experiment in devolution. First of all, there is the fiftieth anniversary of the creation of the Northern Ireland parliament, which falls in 1971. Secondly, the civil disturbances and unrest of recent years have not only cast doubt on the effectiveness of the Stormont administration, but have brought Ireland once more to the forefront of British politics. Thirdly, the growth of Scottish and Welsh nationalist movements has raised the question whether other local parliaments should be established within the United Kingdom, and to this question the experience of Northern Ireland patently has relevance. This is particularly the case since the setting up of the Commission on the Constitution, under the chairmanship of Lord Crowther, in 1968. The commission was charged with the duty of examining 'the present functions of the central legislature and government in relation to the several countries, nations and regions of the United Kingdom', and considering 'whether any changes are desirable in those functions or otherwise in present constitutional and economic relationships'.

Northern Ireland has problems unique to this part of the United Kingdom, and I have sketched in something of the historical and geographical background to show how infertile was the soil in which the devolution experiment was planted. Still, a common justification of devolution is that local administrations should have particular competence in dealing with local problems; it is worth asking why the Northern Ireland system seems to have perpetuated rather than solved its politico-religious problems. The system has changed, as all systems change with the passing of time, and I have aimed to describe the nature of these changes; in this, I have tried to pay as much attention to political realities as to constitutional forms. Northern Ireland is obviously overshadowed by Great Britain, and Stormont by Westminster, but the local administration has been able to pursue a number of independent policies; some of these have been a product of the Protestant-Catholic division, but others have not. On the whole, I have not tried to draw too many conclusions, believing that the events of the past fifty years speak for themselves.

Parts of the book are the product of living and working as a journalist in Northern Ireland, and cannot really be attributed to particular sources. The published works which have been of particular value to me (apart from the many government publications) are Nicholas Mansergh's *The Government of Northern Ireland: A Study in Devolution* (1936); *Ulster Under Home Rule: A Study of the Political and Economic Problems of Northern Ireland,* edited by Thomas Wilson (1955); Denis P. Barritt's and Charles F. Carter's *The Northern Ireland Problem: A Study in Group Relations* (1962); R. J. Lawrence's *The Government of Northern Ireland: Public Finance and Public Services 1921-1964* (1965); and Harry Calvert's *Constitutional Law in Northern Ireland: A Study in Regional Government* (1968). Both the published works and the teaching of E. Estyn Evans, Ireland's most distinguished geographer, helped to shape my understanding of Northern Ireland's problems. The published versions of several series of lectures broadcast by the British Broadcasting Corporation and by Radio Telefis Eireann also provided much information in an easily accessible form. I might add that I am an inveterate collector of newspaper cuttings, which I believe are underrated as a source of historical information.

I have also had the opportunity to read a number of the submissions to the Commission on the Constitution, but I have not really drawn on these for the purposes of this book. I think it is fair to say, though, that in my final chapter I reach conclusions not unlike those reached by Mr C. E. B. Brett. A journalist spends much of his working life picking other people's brains, and to the victims of this operation I owe a debt of gratitude. For the contents of this book, however, I alone bear responsibility.

Finally, I have chosen not to encumber the text with footnotes. At points where I might have done so, the reader will usually be able to find his way to the source of statements or quotations with the help of the bibliography; in some cases, there has obviously been contemporaneous publication in newspapers. Throughout the text, Acts of the Northern Ireland Parliament have been distinguished from Westminster legislation by adding '(NI)'.

Belfast
August 1970

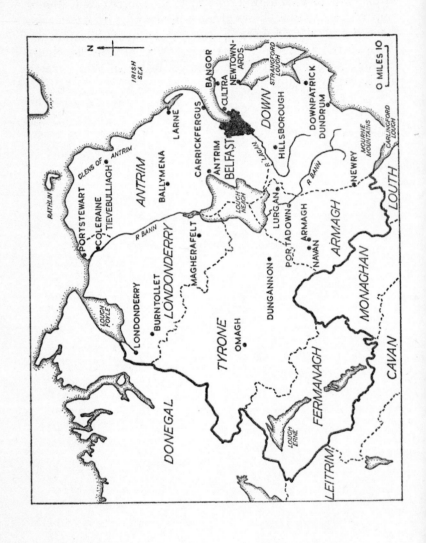

1

The Historical Background

To understand the course of events in Northern Ireland during its years of self-government, it is first necessary to appreciate the historic divisions which led to the establishment of a separate parliament and which continue to overshadow that parliament. In turn, it is necessary to appreciate the separate geographical identity of Northern Ireland—or, rather, of the northern Irish province of Ulster—which has helped to mould its history.

There are nine counties in Ulster, whose name is derived from the Celtic *Uladh*. Six were included in Northern Ireland : Antrim, Down, Armagh, Londonderry, Tyrone and Fermanagh. Three peripheral counties were excluded : Donegal, Cavan and Monaghan. This northern province is separated from Scotland only by a narrow stretch of sea. In its schists, shales and granites, it continues and repeats the outlines of Scottish topography. From prehistoric times there have been close cultural links, whereas the southern part of Ireland has turned more naturally to England and Wales and to the European mainland. The earliest inhabitants of Ireland crossed from Scotland to the north-east county of Antrim, spreading along the coast and up the River Bann to Lough Neagh about 6000 BC. With the melting of the ice which had done so much to sculpt the detail of the northern landscape, Ireland became covered in thick woodland, and the only relics of these Mesolithic or Middle Stone Age people are found along the shores of river, lake and sea. The chalk cliffs of Antrim, capped by black basalt, provided flints which these early food-gatherers shaped as tools. A raised beach at Larne, known as the Curran, contains many of these worked flints.

A readjustment of the levels of land and sea had followed the Ice Age, but by about 2000 BC, when Neolithic or New Stone Age civilisation flourished, the coastline was at about its present level. The new settlers were part of a movement of peoples along the Atlantic coasts of Europe, bringing new techniques of cultivation and livestock-rearing. Pot-making was one of their skills, and leaf-shaped arrowheads record their ability in working flints. Their enduring contribution to the Ulster landscape is the great stone burial chambers which have inspired folk tales through succeeding centuries.

These so-called megalithic monuments fall into two main groups : passage-graves and gallery-graves. Passage-graves consist of a circular chamber reached through a narrow passage; the grave was originally covered by a round pile or cairn of boulders, but in many cases the boulders have been removed. Gallery-graves consist of a long chamber, often divided into segments, with an elongated cairn. The most sophisticated form of gallery-grave is known as a horned cairn or court-grave, and is largely confined to the northern half of the island; the gallery is approached through a forecourt bounded by standing stones arranged in a horn-shaped curve. One of the main concentrations of horned cairns is in the Carlingford Lough area, and they are quite similar to graves found in south-west Scotland. Although the passage-grave is found in Ulster, it is more characteristic of central Ireland, with a notable example at New Grange in the Boyne valley. There is a sharp contrast between the elaborate carved spirals and circles decorating the southern passage-graves and the austerity of the northern gallery-graves. The later Neolithic people also built single-chambered graves known as dolmens, in which a small number of standing stones support a large capstone weighing many tons; like the horned cairn, they are mainly found in northern counties.

Horned cairns are commonly found at elevations of 400-800ft, where light soils could be cultivated more easily than the glacial drifts nearer sea-level. The Neolithic cultivators used polished stone axes to clear woodland, and particularly suitable was the igneous porcellanite or bluestone of county Antrim. Outcrops of porcellanite gave rise to axe factories at

Tievebulliagh and on Rathlin Island, a portent of the north-eastern counties' subsequent dominance in Irish industry.

A knowledge of metal-working reached Ireland around 1800 BC, and bronze implements were soon being exported to Britain. Ulster's industrial and trading experience gave it some advantage; there were workable deposits of copper and gold, and tin was imported. Gold ornaments, such as the crescent-shaped collar or lunula, were also exported. The trading links of southern Ireland were with Cornwall, Brittany and Galicia. Northern links were with Scotland and northern England, with Denmark and Germany, and even Bohemian tin may have been imported. The ornate bowl-shaped Irish food-vessel of the Early Bronze Age reflected the various cultural links with Great Britain. The vase-shaped Yorkshire food-vessel influenced Ulster pottery in the Middle Bronze Age. The bronze rapier became common in this period, but was later supplanted by the leaf-shaped sword which became the model for early iron swords. The Bronze Age, extending over some 1,500 years, has left many monuments. They include stone circles, in some cases aligned to mark the seasons of the year, and isolated standing stones. Some crannogs, artificial lake-dwellings usually built with wooden stakes, brushwood, earth and stones, belong to the Late Bronze Age.

To the succeeding Iron Age belongs the Celtic invasion of Ireland. The period poses many problems for archaeologists, anthropologists and students of language. The Celts had established themselves in central Europe by about 600 BC. Their mastery of iron must have aided their westward migration, and they probably reached Ireland both directly from the European continent and from northern Britain. This is the period of the heroic Irish sagas, and the Celtic horsemen (equipped with chariots in literary sources, though the supporting archaeological evidence is sparse) became a ruling aristocracy. Ulster figures in legend as an area which resisted the invaders most strongly, just as it was to become centuries later the centre of Celtic resistance to the English. Much of Celtic mythology centres on Navan hill-fort or *Emain Macha* (the neck-brooch of Macha), which is close to the present Irish ecclesiastical capital of Armagh (Macha's height). The plan of the fort was supposedly drawn by Queen Macha with a golden

brooch, and the earthwork with surrounding bank was
apparently occupied by the rulers of Ulster from the third
century BC until the fourth century AD. The Ulster cycle of
tales, of which 'The Cattle Raid of Cooley' is most famous, is
centred on the warrior Cuchulain around the first century
AD. The Ulstermen were defeated in the fourth century by
warriors from the western province of Connacht. A prince of
the Connachta, Niall of the Nine Hostages, won fame around
the end of the fourth century by leading raids on Britain,
where the Roman occupation was in its final years. Sons of
Niall established kingdoms in north-west Ulster, with the
dynastic name of Ui Neill or O'Neill.

In origin, the Celts were a nomadic people, and livestock-
rearing came more naturally to them than agriculture. 'The
Cattle Raid of Cooley' begins with Queen Maeve's desire to
possess the finest black bull in Ireland, which, like the white
bull from Connacht which it kills, ultimately appears to have
god-like qualities. But the heroic age yielded to a more settled
occupation of the land, and by the seventh or eighth century
the island was divided into small local kingdoms or *tuatha*.
Meanwhile, Ireland had become a Christian country. Saint
Patrick, who had been brought from Britain to county Antrim
as a boy slave, returned to Ireland in 432 as a bishop bent on
converting the pagans. In 444, Armagh became the centre of
the Irish Church, but the episcopal system never flourished in
a society without towns or villages. Instead, monasteries
became centres, not only of religion and learning, but also of
trading and crafts. In the seventh and eighth centuries, the
golden age of the Irish Church, missionaries spread their
scholarship through Europe.

The commonest archaeological remnants of the period are
raths, circular earthworks 70-150ft in diameter with a bank
and outside ditch. These were farmsteads, and within the
enclosure a low house was usually built; sometimes the whole
area was roofed over, and people and animals lived together.
The king's enclosure would have more than one rampart.
Variants of the rath are the crannog and the cashel, which was
built with dry stone walls where the soil was thin. The pas-
toral tradition remained strong, but the monasteries helped to
encourage tillage and the conquest of the heavier lowland

soils. Ties of kinship were important, and there was a clearly defined class system, from nobles and freemen down to slaves. There were grades of kingship, from the single tuath to a whole province, and tributes were paid. But such Irish unity as existed was cultural rather than political. A learned class survived from pagan times to preserve orally and ultimately to write down epics, poetry, history and the old brehon laws—the brehons were professional jurists—in a native language which the higher clergy ignored in favour of Latin. But the high kings of Tara, which outlasted the rival Emain Macha, commanded no enduring allegiance, and Ireland proved vulnerable to the attacks of Viking longships in the ninth and tenth centuries.

The Vikings or Norsemen began by plundering the countryside, not least the monasteries, which built round towers as look-out points and refuges for the monks and their treasures. Later, they founded trading colonies at Dublin, Wicklow, Wexford, Waterford and elsewhere, establishing urban life for the first time in Ireland. In Ulster, Viking ships sailed up the River Bann to Lough Neagh, but the North offered resistance and destroyed the invaders' settlements. The southern towns survived the defeat of the Vikings by Brian Boru at Clontarf, near Dublin, in 1014. Brian Boru, King of Munster, had usurped the high kingship of Tara, which for centuries had been held by the Ui Neills. But he was killed at Clontarf, and a brief prospect of political unity gave way to internal provincial rivalries which lasted until the Norman invasion.

The Norsemen left little positive mark on Ulster. They destroyed the monastery at Bangor, county Down, which Saint Columbanus had left to found famous monasteries like Luxeuil, in France, and Bobbio, in Italy. They sacked Armagh. They named Strangford and Carlingford loughs and turned the Gaelic *Uladh* into the modern Ulster. Those who settled appear to have been absorbed into the native population.

Similarly, the Normans' impact was limited. Dermot MacMurrough, King of Leinster, had fled from Ireland in 1166 after an unsuccessful intervention in one of the frequent struggles over the high kingship. He offered his allegiance to Henry II, the French King of England, and received in return permission to enlist allies. He found them among the Normans of the Welsh border country; the most important was the Earl of Pembroke, known as Strongbow. The Normans invaded south-east Ireland, and by 1170 had taken Dublin, establishing their military superiority over the Norsemen and the native Irish. A year later, Henry himself arrived with an army, principally to ensure that his barons did not become too powerful in Ireland. It was an unsystematic conquest, and it was left to a young and adventurous knight called John de Courcy to invade Ulster. He captured Downpatrick in 1177, and he and his successors built a number of castles in counties Antrim and Down, the most notable being at Carrickfergus and Dundrum. De Courcy introduced Benedictine monks at Downpatrick, and there are substantial remains of Cistercian abbeys at nearby Inch and at Greyabbey, in the Ards peninsula. But Norman influence did not extend beyond Lough Neagh and the River Bann, and it contracted substantially after the invasion from Scotland by Edward Bruce in 1315.

Bruce was killed in the Battle of Faughart, near Dundalk, in 1318, but by this time he had conquered the north—taking Carrickfergus after a long siege—and the Irish were increasingly able to regain land from the Normans. The de Burgh family succeeded to the 'earldom of Ulster' after the defeat of Bruce, but a family quarrel in 1333 left them unable to impose their authority. Eventually, the Norman conquest of Ulster was reduced to Carrickfergus and footholds in Strangford and Carlingford loughs. In southern Ireland, the Anglo-Norman nobility retained links with England, but Ulster remained a Celtic stronghold and refuge, a primitive region of clans and chieftains. Its bogs and forest were difficult to penetrate. Towns and villages were largely absent, and when the region looked outwards it was across the sea to Scotland rather than to the southern provinces. In turn, Scots settled in Ulster; the most important were the MacDonalds, who became MacDonnells in the nine glens of Antrim.

The sixteenth century brought the Tudor conquest of Ireland. In 1541, following the destruction of the Anglo-Irish house of Kildare, Henry VIII was declared King of Ireland by an Irish parliament summoned for that purpose. For several decades, the earls of Kildare had ruled Ireland as deputies, responsible to the king and taking the place of an absentee lord lieutenant; henceforth, there would always be an Englishman at the head of the administration. Gradually, the Irish chiefs were forced to submit to the English monarchy, surrendering their land and then receiving it back as feudal grants. They agreed to learn English and give up Irish dress; the old Gaelic or Celtic institutions were to be abandoned. The Protestant reformation was introduced to Ireland, though with little ultimate success.

Henry and his successors achieved much by negotiation and occasional force, but Ulster largely retained its independence until the last years of Queen Elizabeth's reign. The Ulster leader was Hugh O'Neill, Earl of Tyrone, a shrewd campaigner who took the title 'The O'Neill' and made an alliance with Hugh Roe O'Donnell to defend the Gaelic tradition. His military successes encouraged rebellion elsewhere in Ireland, threatening the Tudor conquest. Eventually, though, he emerged from familiar northern territory to join an invading Spanish army at Kinsale, county Cork, where he was overwhelmed in 1601. O'Neill finally surrendered in 1603, after Queen Elizabeth's death. He and O'Donnell were allowed to return to their lands, but English authority was now firmly established, and in 1607 they chose to sail into voluntary exile in Europe with more than ninety leading Ulstermen. This 'flight of the earls' left a political vacuum which was filled by the Plantation of Ulster.

With the completion of the Tudor conquest in 1603, traditional Gaelic life yielded to the authority of a Dublin government. English common law replaced brehon law. The Gaelic language remained, however, and the native Irish were further differentiated from their conquerors by religion. But a permanent subjugation of Ulster was now possible, and the new union of England and Scotland under James I widened the area from which settlers could be drawn. In the sixteenth century, attempts to plant English settlers in conquered parts of Munster and Leinster had not been very successful, but the Ulster Plantation was carefully planned and executed.

The lands which the departed earls had claimed to rule were confiscated. These consisted of the counties of Donegal, Coleraine (renamed Londonderry, as was the town of Derry,

B

after the City of London agreed to plant the county), Tyrone, Fermanagh, Armagh and Cavan. Some of the land went to Irishmen, who were to lease it out to tenants and adopt English farming methods. The major plantation was to be executed by 'undertakers', who agreed to bring in Protestant settlers from England and Scotland, to establish towns and villages, and to provide means of defence. Land was also granted to 'servitors', men who had served the Crown in Ireland, and they were free to have Irish tenants. In practice, the undertakers also took Irish tenants, so that many areas were less solidly Protestant than had been intended. Antrim and Down were excluded from the plantation, but individual entrepreneurs managed to plant large areas of north Down and south Antrim with Scottish Presbyterians. Towards the end of the century, the northern Protestants' resistance to the Catholic James II was a prelude to William of Orange's victory at the River Boyne in 1690 and the subsequent buttressing of the Protestant ascendancy throughout Ireland by a series of anti-Catholic penal laws.

Ulster was now differentiated from the rest of Ireland by the numerical strength of the Protestants, but the eighteenth century was well advanced before its political life diverged significantly. Initially, the power of the Episcopalian landlords was dominant, and the Presbyterian tenants suffered civil and political disabilities; there was substantial emigration to America, where the Scotch-Irish played a significant role in the War of Independence. It was the growth of the linen industry in Ulster which brought economic prosperity and subsequently political influence to the Presbyterians, the ways of whose church encouraged independence of thought and democratic action. There was, in addition, the 'Ulster custom', by which northern farmers enjoyed a security of tenure unknown elsewhere and benefitted from improvements they made in their holdings. Finally, the Anglo-Irish landlords determined to secure greater administrative autonomy for the island, and this Protestant nationalism embraced the Presbyterians as well.

Both the American War of Independence and the French Revolution affected the course of events in Ireland. Britain was patently unable to defend the neighbouring island—in

1778, John Paul Jones, the American privateer, captured a British ship in Belfast lough—and there were fears of a French invasion. Volunteer companies were formed locally, and their existence enabled the 'patriot party' to win from a whig government in Britain virtual independence for the Irish parliament. In these events, Ulster played a critical part. The first volunteer company was raised in Belfast; a northern peer, Lord Charlemont, became commander-in-chief of volunteers throughout Ireland. A gathering of volunteers in Dungannon, county Tyrone, in 1782 gave voice to Protestant aspirations better than the parliament in Dublin had done. The formal independence of the Irish parliament was granted later in the year, and lasted until the Act of Union in 1800.

This did not satisfy everyone. The northern Presbyterians were much influenced by American revolutionary ideas, and the fall of the Bastille in Paris was celebrated in Belfast. A Dublin barrister, Theobald Wolfe Tone, published a pamphlet criticising the penal laws, and an alliance between Presbyterians and Catholics seemed possible. In 1791, Tone founded the Society of United Irishmen in Belfast, with the objective of 'an impartial and adequate representation of the Irish nation in parliament'. Two years later, an Act of Parliament gave Catholics the franchise, but they were still not permitted to sit there or to hold government posts. Tone and his colleagues began to contemplate revolution. The situation was aggravated by agrarian unrest and, after an armed battle between Protestants and Catholics in county Armagh in 1795, the Protestant Orange Order was founded. Ulster was close to civil war, and some of the Presbyterian enthusiasm for revolution waned, foreshadowing the ultimate political division between Protestants of all denominations and Catholics. Lord Camden, the lord lieutenant, ordered the disarming of Ulster in 1797, and a rising there and elsewhere the following year was crushed. The rebels were most successful in county Wexford, where some of the Catholic clergy emerged as leaders, but many Protestants were slaughtered by the rebels for apparently sectarian reasons, and this seemed to weaken the resolve of the northern Presbyterians.

The failure of the 1798 rising, soon followed by the creation of a single parliament for Great Britain and Ireland, marked the end of a uniquely liberal period in the history of Ulster, and particularly Belfast. Linen manufacture, introduced by Huguenot refugees and originally a cottage industry, had brought prosperity to the town. The province as a whole was more prosperous than other parts of Ireland—a much smaller proportion of the population were Catholics, demoralised by the penal laws—and the town had a substantial middle class of merchants and shipowners. Presbyterian influence was strong, and their five congregations contrasted with the single parish church. The Presbyterian church was organised on a closely-knit democratic basis; there was a general synod of Ulster, whereas the Episcopalians or churchmen and the Catholics were each part of a system of parishes and dioceses covering the whole island. The Presbyterians suffered just enough disabilities to encourage them to rise above them, and to be both critical of the ruling class of Episcopalian land-owners and sympathetic towards the underprivileged Catho-lics. Scottish influences were strong, not least in the education of Presbyterian clergy and doctors. The overall effect was a burgeoning of social and intellectual life, together with many works of philanthropy. Belfast had its great white linen hall, but it also had its Charitable Society, its Society for Promoting Knowledge (whose first librarian was executed after a short-lived rising in 1803), its academy 'in which the sons of gentlemen who could not conveniently send them to college, might receive a liberal education'. When a Catholic church was opened in the town in 1784, the Belfast Volunteers para-ded in full dress and collected money for the building fund. But the liberalism of this period existed principally among middle-class Presbyterians, and the founding of the Orange Order reflected widespread anti-Catholicism among other northern Protestants.

The Act of Union brought free trade between Great Britain and Ireland, and as linen manufacture became organised on a factory basis Belfast expanded rapidly. In 1800, it had a population of about 20,000; at the 1841 census, the figure was 70,747. More than any other part of Ireland, Belfast paralleled in its own growth the experience of English and Scottish towns of the Industrial Revolution. Shipbuilding became well-established in the 1850s and 1860s, and textile engineering was a natural accompaniment to the linen trade. Industrial development spread to other towns and villages in Ulster, and consequently there was much less of the agrarian disorder which afflicted other parts of Ireland. There was less pressure on land, and less dependence on the potato, so the famine caused by potato blight in 1845-9 had less disastrous effects than elsewhere. Land Acts of 1870 and 1881 put the 'Ulster custom' or 'tenant right' on a statutory basis, and northern farmers generally were satisfied with their treatment at the government's hands. The effect was to remove a potential cause of division within the Protestant community. Similarly, the Disestablishment of the Church of Ireland in 1869 ended a Presbyterian grievance.

Protestant attitudes had also been affected by the success of the struggle for Catholic emancipation. Most of the penal laws had been repealed by the end of the eighteenth century, but Catholics were not permitted to sit at Westminster until 1829. However, they did have the vote before this, and Daniel O'Connell's Catholic Association mobilised this vote with considerable success. Having won the right to sit in parliament, O'Connell went on to campaign for the repeal of the union; Protestants, realising that they would be in a minority in any future Irish parliament, increasingly supported the union. The Orange Order, formed in an area planted with English settlers, began to make more impact on northern Presbyterians. In this, the most influential figure was an intolerant Presbyterian cleric, Henry Cooke; within his own church, he was ultimate victor in a theological battle over freedom of conscience, and more liberal opponents who refused to sign the Westminster Confession of Faith formed a break-away church. Soon after Catholic emancipation was granted, Belfast began to experience the sectarian riots which have since recurred at periods of political crisis.

The most serious riots occurred in 1886, and began a few days before Gladstone's Home Rule Bill was defeated at Westminster. There was also rioting in 1893, after Gladstone had introduced a second Bill, which was also defeated. A third Bill was introduced in 1912; like its predecessors, this Government of Ireland Bill offered only a limited measure of autonomy, but it was strongly opposed by Ulster Protestants.

They were well organised. In 1905, the Ulster Unionist Council had been formed, representing a number of organisations opposed to home rule. In 1912, almost half a million Ulster people signed a covenant to resist home rule by 'all means which may be found necessary'. Plans were made for a provisional government, and the Ulster Volunteer Force was formed; in 1914, a substantial cargo of arms was smuggled into Larne and distributed throughout Ulster.

The Government of Ireland Act became law in 1914 but, because of the outbreak of World War I, it was agreed not to implement it until peace came. In fact, it was never implemented. In 1916, the abortive Easter Rising in Dublin and the subsequent execution of many of its leaders strengthened nationalist feelings in Ireland. In the 1918 general election, the militant Sinn Fein ('Ourselves') movement won 73 of the 105 Irish seats at Westminster. They were committed to abstaining from the British House of Commons, and instead met in Dublin in 1919 as the first *Dail Eireann* ('Assembly of Ireland'). The assembly, ignored by the Unionists and the remnant of the Irish parliamentary party which had pursued home rule by peaceful methods, proclaimed *Saorstat Eireann* ('Free State of Ireland').

There now began a confused and violent period in which two governments claimed to exercise jurisdiction over Ireland. Severe rioting broke out in Belfast in the summer of 1920, and sectarian strife continued there and elsewhere in the North until 1922. The guerilla tactics of the Irish Republican Army (more often abbreviated to IRA) undoubtedly heightened Protestant animosity, and many Catholics were killed or lost their homes as a result. The British Prime Minister, David Lloyd George, had proposed after the 1916 rising that the Home Rule Act should come into operation before the war ended, but with six Ulster counties excluded. Negotiations came to nothing; the Unionist leader, Sir Edward Carson, would have accepted the proposal as a permanent solution but the leader of the Irish parliamentary party, John Redmond, would only agree to a temporary partition of the island. However, the idea of partition had been mooted, and in 1920 the British Government under Lloyd George opted for it as the best compromise between conflicting demands. The new Government of Ireland Act became law in December 1920.

In theory, the Act provided for the eventual unification of the island, as the summary of its main provisions pointed out :

> Although at the beginning there are to be two Parliaments and two Governments in Ireland, the Act contemplates and affords every facility for Union between North and South, and empowers the two Parliaments by mutual agreement and joint action to terminate partition and to set up one Parliament and one Government for the whole of Ireland.

The Act provided for a Council of Ireland consisting of twenty representatives of each parliament, but with very restricted powers, although it could make suggestions for joint action by the two parliaments. Its president was to be nominated by the lord lieutenant. In fact, the council never functioned. Although a general election was held in both parts of Ireland, only four members of the southern House of Commons attended the opening of parliament in Dublin on 28 June 1921. The 124 unopposed Sinn Fein candidates had regarded the election as determining the membership of the second Dail. In July, negotiations began between the British Government and the Sinn Fein leaders, and on 6 December 1921 the Anglo-Irish Treaty (strictly speaking, entitled 'Articles of agreement for a treaty between Great Britain and Ireland') was signed in London.

The treaty provided for the Irish Free State to become a self-governing dominion within 'the Community of Nations known as the British Empire', and its members of parliament were to take an oath of allegiance to the Crown. The treaty provided for a governor-general, as in other British dominions, and Britain retained some naval establishments within the twenty-six counties which formed the Irish Free State. So far as the six north-eastern counties of Northern Ireland were concerned, the important provision of the treaty was that the parliament and government of the Irish Free State should not exercise jurisdiction there until one month after the treaty was ratified by Act of Parliament. Within this month, the two houses of the Northern Ireland Parliament could—and did—present an address to the King to exclude the six counties from the Irish Free State. In such circumstances, the treaty provided for the establishment of a boundary commission to 'determine in accordance with the wishes of the inhabitants, so far as may be compatible with economic and geographic conditions, the boundaries between Northern Ireland and the rest of Ireland'.

The address to the King was passed on 17 December 1922, but the boundary commission was not appointed until 31 October 1924. The treaty had provided that the governments of Northern Ireland and the Irish Free State should each appoint one commissioner, and that the British Government should appoint a chairman. However, the Northern Ireland Government took the view that a final settlement had been reached, and refused to make an appointment. A supplementary agreement between the other two governments on 4 August 1924 allowed the British Government to appoint J. R. Fisher as the Northern Ireland member; he was a former editor of the *Northern Whig*, a Belfast newspaper committed to the Unionist cause. The chairman was Mr Justice Feetham of the South African Supreme Court, and the southern nominee Professor Eoin MacNeill, the Minister of Education.

The southern signatories of the treaty had been confident that a boundary commission which took account of 'the wishes of the inhabitants' would recommend the transfer of substantial portions of the six counties to the Irish Free State. Michael Collins, one of the southern leaders, had written : 'We would save Tyrone and Fermanagh, parts of Derry, Armagh and Down by the Boundary Commission; the North would be forced economically to come in'. However, the phrasing of the treaty allowed for a restrictive interpretation, and Feetham adopted this in a memorandum submitted to his colleagues. His words were repeated in the commission's draft report :

> Northern Ireland must, when the boundaries have been determined, still be recognisable as the same provincial entity; the changes made must not be so drastic as to destroy its identity or make it impossible for it to continue as a separate province of the United Kingdom with its own parliament and government for provincial affairs under the Government of Ireland Act.

On 5 November 1925, the commissioners approved a first

draft of their award. It proposed including some border areas of Tyrone, Fermanagh and Armagh in the Irish Free State, and also parts of Donegal and Monaghan in Northern Ireland. Two days later, a London newspaper, the *Morning Post*, published a fairly accurate forecast and map of the proposals. Public opinion in the Irish Free State was shocked and MacNeill, probably under pressure from his own government, resigned from the commission on 20 November. It now seemed unlikely that any award made by the remaining commissioners could be enforced, and after further negotiations between the three governments it was agreed on 3 December that the existing boundary should remain unchanged. Meanwhile, Feetham and Fisher—who had originally hoped to publish a unanimous award without an accompanying report detailing evidence and arguments—withheld their signatures from the draft award, but insisted on submitting on 9 December a report showing how the boundaries would have been determined. This remained secret until 1968.

One effect of the agreement of 3 December 1925 was that the Council of Ireland was formally dissolved on 1 April 1926. It only remained for Westminster to repeal, in 1927, those parts of the Government of Ireland Act which related to Southern Ireland. In 1937, the Irish Free State adopted a new constitution which in theory applied to the whole of Ireland; however, its jurisdiction was limited to the twenty-six counties 'pending the reintegration of the national territories'. But, while no Irish vote had been cast in favour of the partition contained in the Government of Ireland Act of 1920, the exclusion of part of Ireland from the Irish Free State had since been endorsed in principle by the 1921 treaty, the 1924 agreement providing for Fisher's appointment to the boundary commission, and the 1925 agreement signed 'in a spirit of neighbourly comradeship'.

In 1936, the Dublin parliament passed the External Affairs Act; the British monarch ceased to be the titular head of the Irish Free State, but was recognised as an instrument for validating the accreditation of Irish diplomats. In 1949, the Irish Free State formally became the Republic of Ireland and ceased to belong to the British Commonwealth. In turn, section 1(2) of the Ireland Act of 1949 at Westminster gave a firm and specific guarantee of Northern Ireland's constitutional position :

It is hereby declared that Northern Ireland remains part of His Majesty's dominions and of the United Kingdom and it is hereby affirmed that in no event will Northern Ireland or any part thereof cease to be part of His Majesty's dominions and of the United Kingdom without the consent of the Parliament of Northern Ireland.

2

Political Institutions

The first prime minister of Northern Ireland was Sir James Craig, later Viscount Craigavon. He entered the British House of Commons in 1906, and during the debate on the Government of Ireland Bill in 1920 he admitted that the Unionist majority in the nine counties of Ulster was very small. 'We admit quite frankly that we cannot hold the nine counties. Therefore we decided that, in the interests of the greater part of Ulster, it is better we should give up the three counties.' The 1920 Act is, in effect, the constitution of Northern Ireland. It was modified by the 1922 Irish Free State (Consequential Provisions) Act to take account of the emergence of the new dominion, but its essential structure has remained intact.

The legislature

The legislature consists of the Crown, the House of Commons and the Senate. The 1922 Act abolished the office of lord lieutenant, and the Crown's representative in Northern Ireland is now the governor. It is his duty to summon, prorogue (that is, discontinue meetings between sessions) and dissolve parliament in the Monarch's name. He also grants or withholds royal assent to legislation passed by both houses of parliament, subject to certain limitations. These are that he must comply with any instructions given by the monarch in respect of a Bill and, if so directed, must reserve a Bill. A reserved Bill does not become law until royal assent is granted, and lapses if assent is not granted within one year. Only once has a Bill been reserved, but there was a sharp reaction from the Northern Ireland Parliament, and royal assent to the

27

Local Government Bill (NI), 1922, was not long delayed; the Bill provided for the abolition of proportional representation in council elections. In 1970, opposition MPs and senators petitioned the Governor, Lord Grey of Naunton, to withhold royal assent to the Public Order (Amendment) Bill (NI). The petition was rejected after the governor had consulted the Home Office in London and been informed that the home secretary had no special instruction to convey from the Queen nor any direction that the governor should reserve the Bill.

The governor holds office for a term of six years, but can be reappointed—as was the first holder of the office, the Duke of Abercorn. His official residence is Government House at Hillsborough, county Down. The 1920 Act provides that no one should be disqualified from holding the office (originally of lord lieutenant) on account of religious belief, but no Catholic has been appointed governor and not until 1964 was a Presbyterian, Lord Erskine of Rerrick, appointed. The office carries a salary of £4,000 ($9,600), with an expenses allowance of up to £10,000 ($24,000). An additional power, which no governor has had to use, is to convene a joint sitting of the Commons and Senate. This could arise if the Senate rejected or failed to pass a Bill sent to it by the Commons, or if it passed it with amendments to which the Commons would not agree. If the Bill were again sent to the Senate in the next session of Parliament, and again agreement was not reached, the governor could convene a joint sitting. A majority vote of the MPs and senators present would then decide the outcome of the Bill and the individual amendments. So far, the Senate has not often rejected legislation approved by the Commons, and when this has happened the Commons has yielded.

There are fifty-two seats in the Northern Ireland House of Commons. Originally these were divided into multi-member constituencies, with election by proportional representation on the single transferable vote system; four MPs represented the Queen's University constituency, and the remainder territorial constituencies with four to eight MPs each. Section 14(5) of the Government of Ireland Act gave the new parliament the right to alter 'the qualification and registration of the electors, the law relating to elections and the question of elections, the constituencies, and the distribution of the members among the constituencies' after three years from its first meeting (which was on 7 June 1921). However, the number of seats could not be altered, and any redistribution of seats had to take account of population. In 1929, under the House of Commons (Method of Voting and Redistribution of Seats) Act (NI), proportional representation was abolished and single-member constituencies were introduced except in the university constituency. Lord Craigavon justified the change in these words :

> At election times, the people do not really understand what danger may result if they make a mistake when it comes to third, fourth, fifth or sixth preferences. By an actual mistake, they might wake up to find Northern Ireland in the perilous position of being submerged in a Dublin parliament.

The university seats were abolished under the Electoral Law (Amendment) Act (NI), 1968, and the consequent provision of four more territorial seats made possible a redrawing of boundaries to take account of population growth on the periphery of Belfast. The boundary commission set up for this purpose was asked also to make subsequent recommendations for Northern Ireland as a whole.

The same act also abolished the business vote. Hitherto, an elector could claim one additional vote if he occupied business premises with a rateable value of £10 ($24) in another constituency. It was thus possible, if he was also a graduate, to vote in three constituencies and to be represented by six MPs. In 1969, the Electoral Law (No. 2) Act (NI), lowered the voting age from 21 to 18. Although the Government of Ireland Act, 1920, provided that the franchise for the United Kingdom and Northern Ireland parliaments should initially be the same, differences emerged after the Northern Ireland Parliament became free in 1924 to go its own way. The principal remaining differences are the residential and nationality qualifications. British subjects and citizens of the Republic of Ireland are entitled to be on the Westminster register of voters, subject to a qualifying period of residence of three months. Only British subjects are entitled to be on the register for the Northern Ireland Parliament, and they must have been born in Northern Ireland or have resided continuously in the

United Kingdom during the seven years preceding the qualifying date.

The House of Commons is elected for a period of five years,
unless sooner dissolved. Members are elected by a simple
majority, and candidates who receive less than one-eighth of
the votes cast in their constituency forfeit a deposit of £150
($360). A member of the Commons cannot also belong to the
Senate, but a government minister can sit and speak in both
houses, provided that he votes only in the one to which he
belongs. Unlike Westminster, peers are not excluded from the
House of Commons; two former prime ministers, Lord Craigavon and Lord Brookeborough, were entitled to sit in the
British House of Lords. It is also possible to sit in both houses
of commons, and this has happened in a few cases. Salaries
are fixed by resolution of the House of Commons, and since
1965 have been £1,450 ($3,480) per year with expenses of £300
($720) for MPs who are not paid as members of the govern-
ment or as officers of the house. Both the Commons and the
Senate meet at Stormont, on the outskirts of Belfast.

There are twenty-six seats in the Northern Ireland Senate.
The lord mayor of Belfast and the mayor of Londonderry are
ex-officio members, and the other twenty-four senators are
elected by MPs under a system of proportional representation.
Senators are elected for a term of eight years, and half of the
elected senators retire every fourth year. The dissolution of
parliament thus does not affect the political composition of
the Senate, and in theory the balance of parties in the two
chambers could be substantially different; if the Unionist
party were to lose control of the Commons at a future general
election, Unionist senators could well be in a position to block
legislation (even in a joint sitting of the two houses). In
practice, the Senate has tended to be a pale reflection of the
Commons, and (like the House of Lords) commonly has a
number of former MPs. There was no provision for an upper
chamber in the Government of Ireland Bill when it was introduced at Westminster in 1920, and the Senate was created
under an amendment initiated in the House of Lords. Earlier
home rule Bills had proposed a variety of two-chamber
legislatures for Ireland, and suggested franchises for an upper
chamber had included the hereditary principle, nomination

and the election of regional representatives; in practice, the choice of Unionist senators tends to reflect regional interests. The *Seanad* or Senate in the Republic of Ireland is largely composed of members elected to represent vocational and cultural interests and the universities, and on occasions it has been suggested that the composition of the Northern Ireland Senate should be re-examined. Senators receive a salary of £600 ($1,440) per year and a daily attendance allowance of £2.25 ($5.40) where they are not paid as members of the government or as officers of the house.

Under section 4(1) of the Government of Ireland Act, 1920, the Northern Ireland Parliament has power to pass laws for 'the peace, order and good government of Northern Ireland', subject only to certain specific limitations. Essentially, this position has remained, although there have been a number of amending Acts to deal with problems not envisaged in the original legislation. In 1928, for example, the Northern Ireland (Miscellaneous Provisions) Act provided power to make 'regulations as to standards of quality, inspection or compulsory insurance' governing the export of livestock or agricultural produce to other parts of the British Isles. Hitherto, it had seemed that legislation affecting external trade might be ruled out by the provision in section 4(1) that 'they shall not have power to make laws except in respect of matters exclusively relating to the portion of Ireland within their jurisdiction, or some part thereof'. Similarly, section 1 of the Northern Ireland Act, 1947, provided power to pass legislation covering cross-border schemes concerned with water power, the storage and supply of water, drainage and irrigation, electricity supply, roads, railways, inland waterways and bridges.

The fact that the Northern Ireland Parliament can only legislate in matters within its own territory distinguishes it from sovereign parliaments such as Westminster or those in British dominions, which can regulate the actions of their citizens while abroad. In addition, section 4(1) sets out a number of 'excepted matters' on which the Northern Ireland Parliament has no power to legislate. These include the Crown, peace and war, the armed forces, treaties with foreign states, titles of honour, treason, treatment of aliens and natu-

ralisation, external trade, submarine cables, wireless tele-
graphy, aerial navigation, lighthouses, coinage and banknotes,
trademarks, copyright and patent rights.

The 1920 Act also sets out a number of 'reserved matters'
which it was originally intended to transfer to an all-Ireland
parliament. These include the postal service, the Post Office
Savings Bank and trustee savings banks, the design of stamps,
the Public Record Office of Ireland, certain matters relating
to land purchase, a number of important taxes, and the
Supreme Court in Northern Ireland. The reserved taxes under
the Act are customs and excise duty, excess profits duty, corporation profits tax, any other tax on profits, income tax
(including supertax), and any tax substantially the same in
character as any of these. In addition, the Northern Ireland
Parliament was prohibited from imposing any tax 'of the
nature of a general tax upon capital, not being a tax substantially the same in character as an existing tax'. Again there
has been amending legislation. In 1928, for example, the
Northern Ireland (Miscellaneous Provisions) Act gave the
Northern Ireland Parliament power to confer jurisdiction on
the Supreme Court 'to hear and determine appeals from, and
questions of law on cases stated for its opinion by, any inferior
court or other tribunal'. In 1935, the Northern Ireland Land
Purchase (Winding Up) Act largely de-reserved land purchase.
Moreover, the 1920 Act included specific permission for the
establishment of a public record office for Northern Ireland,
and appropriate legislation was passed in 1923.

Section 5(1) of the Government of Ireland Act, 1920, contains important prohibitions in the fields of religious discrimination and the confiscation of property :

> In the exercise of their power to make laws under this Act
> neither the Parliament of Southern Ireland nor the Parlia-
> ment of Northern Ireland shall make a law so as either
> directly or indirectly to establish or endow any religion, or
> prohibit or restrict the free exercise thereof, or give a pref-
> erence, privilege, or advantage, or impose any disability or
> disadvantage, on account of religious belief or religious or
> ecclesiastical status, or make any religious belief or religious
> ceremony a condition of the validity of any marriage, or
> affect prejudicially the right of any child to attend a school
> receiving public money without attending the religious in-

struction at that school, or alter the constitution of any religious body except where the alteration is approved on behalf of the religious body by the governing body thereof, or divert from any religious denomination the fabric of cathedral churches, or, except for the purposes of roads, railways, lighting, water, or drainage works, or other works of public utility upon payment of compensation, any other property, or take any property without compensation.

The prohibition on taking property without compensation was abolished by section 14 of the Northern Ireland Act, 1962, but it can still be used to challenge the validity of legislation passed earlier. There was, however, a retrospective validation of legislation 'providing security of tenure for, or enlarging the estates or interests in land of, persons or any class of persons'. The 1962 Act also made provision for the compulsory acquisition of land (on payment of compensation) from a religious denomination or educational institution for housing, slum clearance, and development or redevelopment, with the exception of buildings occupied and used exclusively for religious or educational purposes. The Act also ensured that laws providing for control of the use of land could be applied to property owned by a religious denomination or educational institution. Clearly, there is ambiguity in the prohibition of laws 'either directly or indirectly to establish or endow any religion', which arguably could rule out aid to religious institutions even on a non-discriminatory basis. The issue arises most obviously in connection with aid to 'voluntary schools' which profess religious objectives, and which receive state aid.

In practice, there has been a harmonious relationship between the United Kingdom and Northern Ireland parliaments, and Westminster has been prepared to pass legislation clarifying the powers of the subordinate parliament or extending them in response to situations not envisaged in the 1920 Act. Where Westminster has legislated on 'transferred matters', it has been with the consent of the Northern Ireland Government. Under section 6(1) of the 1920 Act, United Kingdom statutes and all other laws existing in Ireland at 3 May 1921 continued in force, but could be amended or repealed by the new parliament where they concerned trans-

C

ferred matters; where more recent Westminster legislation embraces matters within the power of the Northern Ireland Parliament, it commonly contains a provision deeming it to be an Act passed before 3 May 1921.

The absolute sovereignty of Westminster is, however, fully protected by section 75 of the 1920 Act.

> Notwithstanding the establishment of the Parliament of . . . Northern Ireland . . . or anything contained in this Act, the supreme authority of the Parliament of the United Kingdom shall remain unaffected and undiminished over all persons, matters and things in [Northern] Ireland and every part thereof.

On 9 August 1966, Miss Alice Bacon, Minister of State at the Home Office, told the Commons at Westminster that there could be no question of the British Government interfering in matters transferred to Stormont without legislation passed by virtue of section 75. She said the section preserved the supreme authority of the United Kingdom Parliament, but not of the government, over transferred matters. However, on 25 October 1967, the British Home Secretary, Mr Roy Jenkins, noted that while Northern Ireland existed because of its desire to be part of the United Kingdom 'that unity can have little meaning unless we work towards common economic and social standards and common standards in political tolerance and non-discrimination on both sides of the Irish Sea'. The inter-governmental discussions following the civil disturbances of August 1969 in Northern Ireland indicated that, in fact, the British Government could exert a substantial or even dominant influence in transferred matters.

There are procedures for determining if Stormont legislation is *ultra vires*—that is, beyond the powers of the Northern Ireland Parliament and therefore void. Under section 51 of the 1920 Act, there is provision for a Bill or an Act to be referred to the Judicial Committee of the Privy Council, a committee which acts as a final court of appeal from courts in many parts of the British Commonwealth. If the committee finds that any part of the legislation is *ultra vires*, its decision is binding. Initially, the governor or a secretary of state (presumably the home secretary) makes a representation to 'His Majesty in Council', after which—'if His Majesty so directs'—the issue is referred to the committee. The procedure was utilised in 1936, when Belfast Corporation petitioned the governor, contending that an education levy imposed on local authorities by section 3 of the Finance Act (NI), 1934, was substantially the same as an income tax. The governor forwarded the petition to the home secretary, who, judging that (as the 1920 Act provided) it was 'expedient in the public interest that steps shall be taken for the speedy determination of the question', made the necessary representation. The committee decided that a levy on rates was not a tax.

A commoner occurrence is for the validity of an Act to be questioned during ordinary litigation. In this instance, under sections 49 and 50 of the 1920 Act, there is a right of appeal to the Northern Ireland Court of Appeal and (with its permission) beyond this to the House of Lords. One safeguard against Stormont inadvertently overstepping its powers is the close liaison between civil servants of the British and Northern Ireland governments. In addition, when a Bill is presented to the governor for royal assent, it must be accompanied by a certificate from the attorney-general indicating that the Bill does not infringe the 1920 Act. The courts, when judging the validity of Northern Ireland Acts, employ the 'pith and substance' doctrine, whereby legislation is not ruled invalid if it marginally and incidentally goes beyond Stormont's competence. The doctrine as applied in Northern Ireland was well illustrated by the case of Gallagher v Lynn, which arose from the Milk and Milk Products Act (NI), 1934. The Act imposed hygienic controls on the sale of milk 'to protect the health of the inhabitants of Northern Ireland', and one effect was to inhibit the import of milk from the Irish Free State. External trade is an excepted matter under the 1920 Act, but the legislation was not ruled *ultra vires*. In a House of Lords judgement in 1937, Lord Atkin said :

> It is well established that you are to look at . . . 'the pith and substance of the legislation'. If, on the view of the statute as a whole, you find that the substance of the legislation is within the express powers, then it is not invalidated if incidentally it affects matters which are outside the authorised field.

Parliamentary practices at Stormont are largely modelled

on those at Westminster, and little use has been made of power under the 1920 Act to pass legislation dealing with the powers, privileges and immunities of Parliament. The programme of legislation and other business is set out in the Queen's Speech, which is read by the governor at the beginning of each parliamentary session. Legislation passes through the same stages as at Westminster. A formal first reading is followed by a second reading, the debate on which covers the general principles of the Bill; amendments are taken at the committee stage and again at the report stage before the Bill is given a third reading. The small size of the chambers at Stormont means the committee stage is taken by a committee consisting of the full Commons or Senate. The large majority of Bills are introduced in the Commons rather than the Senate, and under section 16 of the 1920 Act 'Bills imposing taxation or appropriating revenue or moneys' must do so. The Senate has no power to amend money Bills. The provision for private Bills shows some variation from Westminster practice, with a single committee stage taken by a small committee drawn from both chambers. There are fewer standing committees than at Westminster, and these are commonly joint committees of both chambers—for example, the joint select committee on statutory rules, orders and regulations. Stormont further differs from Westminster in being essentially a part-time parliament. The House of Commons normally meets only on three afternoons each week—the Senate less often—and is in recess for substantial periods at Christmas, Easter and particularly summer. One effect is that the executive arm of government is probably more dominant, relatively speaking, than at Westminster. This is reinforced by the fact that a much higher proportion of the governing party holds government office, and possibly also by the fact that one party has held power since 1921.

The executive

Under British constitutional law, executive power is vested in the monarch and exercised on the monarch's behalf by ministers of the Crown. This was affirmed in section 8 of the 1920 Act, which provided that the lord lieutenant might exercise on the monarch's behalf any prerogative or other executive power delegated to him. Letters patent were issued on 27 April 1921 to constitute the office of lord lieutenant of Ireland, who was authorised to 'do and execute all things which by the right, usage, and custom of Ireland have heretofore appertained to the office of Lord Lieutenant' or which might appertain to the office in consequence of the 1920 Act. The Irish Free State (Consequential Provisions) Act, 1922, transferred these powers to the newly created office of governor, for which letters patent were issued on 9 December 1922. The governor is appointed by the Crown, acting on the advice of the British Government, but it is customary to consult the Northern Ireland Government. The governor, in turn, appoints the ministers in charge of the various government departments; this is a purely formal procedure, except that circumstances might arise in which he had to exercise his discretion in appointing a prime minister.

In 1921, before parliament met for the first time, the lord lieutenant used his power under section 8 of the 1920 Act to establish the Prime Minister's Department and the ministries of Finance, Home Affairs, Labour, Education, Commerce and Agriculture. A seventh ministry, Public Security, existed from 1940 till 1944, when its functions were assumed by the Ministry of Home Affairs. The Ministry of Health and Local Government was established by the Ministries Act (NI), 1944, which also empowered the governor to transfer functions from one department to another and to alter the names of departments. In 1964, the ministries of Labour and National Insurance (as it had become in 1946) and of Health and Local Government were reorganised into the ministries of Health and Social Services and of Development, the latter also taking over some Home Affairs functions. A Ministry of Community Relations was created in 1969.

The heads of departments are designated ministers, and each must be a member of the Commons or the Senate or become one within six months. All or most of the departmental ministers normally hold seats in the Commons, and the practice is to appoint a minister in the Senate. Section 8 (4) of the 1920 Act provided for the appointment of non-departmental ministers who were not required to sit in

Parliament, but there have been none so far. All ministers become members of the Privy Council of Northern Ireland, and they form what is termed the Executive Committee of the Privy Council—commonly known as the Cabinet. With the growth of departmental business, the number of junior government appointments has tended to increase. These are usually posts as parliamentary secretary; there is no firm pattern to these appointments, and their existence seems to depend partly on the pressure of departmental business and the capacity of the minister to deal with it. The chief whip of the governing party normally holds a parliamentary secretary-ship in Finance. The Westminster office of minister of state was introduced in 1966; in a government reshuffle, the Minister of Home Affairs, Mr R. W. B. McConnell, became Minister of State at the Ministry of Development, a lesser demotion than being reduced to the rank of parliamentary secretary. He retained cabinet rank as did the newly appointed leader of the House of Commons, who arranges the chamber's programme of work; hitherto, this office had usually been carried out by the minister of finance. With the creation of the Ministry of Community Relations in 1969, the government drew from the Commons eleven cabinet ministers, three par-liamentary secretaries and the attorney-general; two other members of the governing Unionist Party were officers of the House of Commons, namely the speaker and his deputy, the chairman of ways and means. Thus, almost half of the thirty-six official Unionist MPs held paid offices, and the proportion could be much higher in a more narrowly divided house.

The prime minister's salary was fixed in 1965 at £5,750 ($13,800). Ministerial heads of departments receive £4,250 ($10,200), and the attorney-general £4,750 ($11,400). Other government salaries are within the range £1,750-£3,500 ($4,200-$8,400). The effective power to appoint and dismiss members of the government rests with the prime minister, on whose advice the governor acts. The principle of collective responsibility operates, whereby all members of the cabinet are obliged to express support for all cabinet policies, but it is observed with some leniency; this perhaps reflects the Unionists' dominance of Parliament, which means that much of the effective discussion of political issues must be carried on openly by Unionists. Nonetheless, on 11 December 1968 Capt Terence O'Neill called for the resignation of his Minister of Home Affairs, Mr William Craig, because—as the prime minister wrote to him—'you chose to dispute my views on Section 75 of the Government of Ireland Act and to say that any use of Westminster's sovereign powers under that Section should be "resisted" '. On 10 December, Mr Craig had spoken about section 75 at a Unionist rally in Belfast, saying,

> I would resist any effort by any government in Great Britain, whatever its complexion might be, to exercise that power in any way to interfere with the proper jurisdiction of the Government of Northern Ireland. It is merely a reserve of power to deal with an emergency situation. It is difficult to envisage any situation in which it could be exercised without the consent of the Government of Northern Ireland.

The prime minister affirmed that the attorney-general, the government's principal adviser on constitutional matters, did not agree with Mr Craig's views.

Initially, even ministerial office could be considered a part-time occupation; Sir James Craig, in forming his first administration, was thus able to call on talents which might not otherwise have been available to him. The increasing burden of legislation and administration since World War II, however, has compelled ministers to spend more time in their departments. In June 1963, Capt O'Neill set out a code of conduct for ministers not dissimilar to one promulgated at Westminster by Sir Winston Churchill in 1952 :

> 1. The basic principle is that no Minister should place himself in such a position that his private interests may conflict with his public duty. It follows that he should not engage in any activities which are incompatible, or which might interfere with the full and impartial discharge of his official duty.
> 2. Thus:
> (a) A Minister should avoid any business interest which is sufficiently direct and substantial to exert or appear to be likely to exert an influence on the impartial performance of his public duties
> (b) A Minister should avoid a business interest of a direct and substantial nature involving, or likely to involve, a contract for the supply of goods or services to or by any department of the Government of Northern Ireland.

    (c) A Minister should avoid any outside interest which makes such demands upon his time and energies that it becomes difficult for him properly to discharge the prior responsibilities of his public office.

3. A Minister should not use for pecuniary or other private advantage privileged information to which he has access by virtue of his official position.

4. Where it is proper for a Minister to retain any private interest, it is the rule that he should declare that interest to his colleagues if they have to discuss public business in any way affecting it, and that he should entirely detach himself from the consideration of that business.

5. Within these rules, however, it is obviously desirable that Ministers should not be prevented merely because they hold Ministerial office from receiving such form of grants or subsidies as they would qualify for in the same way as other members of the public. In such cases it must be clear that Ministers do not derive any special advantage from their special position.

6. The application of these principles is the personal responsibility of each Minister, but in any case of doubt the Prime Minister of the day must be the final judge. Ministers should, therefore, submit any such case to him for his direction.

7. In this context, Ministers include all members of the Government.

The code is less restrictive than its Westminster counterpart, in allowing ministers to retain directorships, details of which are published at intervals. Capt O'Neill dismissed his Minister of Agriculture, Mr Harry West, on 26 April 1967 for an alleged breach of the code. The issue involved Mr West's purchase of land which it was possible might subsequently be publicly acquired for an airport; quite apart from the technical issues involved, the prime minister took the view that Mr West had not accepted his direction (as provided for in paragraph 6) and had committed a 'breach of the clear undertaking given to the Attorney-General and myself'. There were, however, other political differences between the two men, and Mr West subsequently spoke of his 'solemn conviction that a deliberate attempt had been made to discredit me in the House and in the eyes of the public'.

Both the dismissals of Mr Craig and Mr West and the softening of the demotion of Mr McConnell illustrate the difficulty of making ministerial changes (except by a simple reshuffle) in a small parliament without creating personal animosities. The Unionists have not experienced periods in opposition, at the end of which a new prime minister could construct a fresh-looking administration. Changes of party leadership might be more readily accomplished in periods of opposition following electoral defeat; in fact, each of Northern Ireland's first four prime ministers ended his term of office amid mounting criticism. Craigavon died in November 1940, not many months after two junior members of the government resigned because they felt the war effort was being ineffectively fostered. His successor was Mr J. M. Andrews, a cabinet minister since 1921, and there was continuing criticism until he resigned in 1943. His successor was Sir Basil Brooke, later Viscount Brookeborough, who revitalised the cabinet by getting rid of its long-serving members; at the end of Lord Brookeborough's period in office, there was criticism of his failure to deal with Northern Ireland's economic problems. Capt O'Neill became prime minister in March 1963, and endured a number of leadership crises before deciding to resign in April 1969, when his position was becoming untenable; at that point, Mr Craig and Mr West were among his leading critics within the Unionist Party. Neither man found a place in the administration formed by O'Neill's successor, Major James Chichester-Clark, and they were among five Unionist MPs who were expelled from the Unionist parliamentary party when on 18 March 1970 they refused to support a House of Commons motion of confidence in the government and its policies.

The 1920 Act made provision for the transfer of civil servants from the existing departments in Ireland to the new Northern Ireland government. These men formed the nucleus of the new civil service, and possibly had a greater breadth of outlook than successors who were recruited directly into the service. In 1923, an order by the governor appointed the minister of finance and two permanent officials as civil service commissioners. The Ministry of Finance is responsible for making regulations governing such matters as recruitment, salaries and conditions of work. In the early years, particular preference was given to ex-servicemen. Recruitment is nor-

mally by open competition, with the administrative grades
being filled in much the same way as in the British civil
service. The proportion of Catholics in the higher grades has
always been small, but this is not necessarily evidence of discrimination, since Catholics have traditionally opposed
Northern Ireland's separate existence. However, following the
disturbances in August 1969, a joint working party of the
British and Northern Ireland governments was set up to
review the adequacy of measures taken to prevent discrimination in public employment. In a communique issued on 10
October 1969, during the visit to Northern Ireland of the
Home Secretary, Mr James Callaghan, it was stated :

> The Joint Working Party found that the Civil Service of
> Northern Ireland deservedly enjoys a high reputation for
> fairness and impartiality in its employment practices and is
> open to criticism in only a few minor aspects. Action will be
> taken in respect of these. The powers of the Northern Ireland
> Parliamentary Commissioner for Administration will be
> extended to personnel matters in the Civil Service.

At that time, none of the permanent departmental heads was
a Catholic, but Mr Patrick Shea became permanent secretary
in Education in December 1969; another Catholic, Mr
Bonaparte Wyse, was the second occupant of the post in 1927.
Also in December 1969, an order was made reconstituting the
civil service commission. The minister of finance ceased to be
a member, and instead there was a five-man body whose
chairman was the head of the civil service. The other members
were two permanent secretaries, a senior professional officer
(an architect), and the head of the newly created civil service
management division. The order laid down that, in filling
posts, 'the order of merit of the applicants is to be fairly and
impartially determined'.

The post of parliamentary commissioner for administration,
or ombudsman, was foreshadowed in the Unionist reform
programme of 22 November 1968, which was an attempt to
meet some of the demands of the civil rights movement. The
necessary legislation was passed in 1969, and the first ombudsman was Sir Edmund Compton, who held a similar post in
relation to departments of the British Government (including
any operations they might have in Northern Ireland). The

ombudsman's task is to investigate allegations of maladministration by government departments; complaints must be referred to him by an MP.

Westminster

In addition to Stormont, the Northern Ireland electorate is represented by twelve MPs at Westminster. Under the Redistribution of Seats (Ireland) Act, 1918, the six counties had thirty members, but this was reduced to thirteen under the 1920 Act on the reasoning that a subordinate legislature was taking over much of the MPs' work. The university seat was abolished, along with similar seats in Great Britain, in 1948. Under the House of Commons (Redistribution of Seats) Act, 1949, a boundary commission is charged with the duty of reviewing the constituencies.

The reduction in representation at Westminster has not merely diminished Northern Ireland's voice in national affairs; it has also had the effect of diminishing the electorate's interest in these affairs. The existence of a local parliament has further accentuated this trend, and politics have tended to be concerned with narrow issues, particularly the constitutional issue of whether or not Northern Ireland is to remain part of the United Kingdom. The Unionists have always held at least eight of the twelve seats at Westminster, where they accept the Conservative whip. They have seemed to represent not merely their constituents, but also the Northern Ireland Government, defending it when necessary against criticisms of conditions in Northern Ireland from Labour and Liberal MPs.

The Northern Ireland MPs are full members of the British House of Commons, but it has been argued sometimes that they should not take part or vote in debates on such matters as housing, education and local government. MPs representing constituencies in Great Britain have no direct influence on the conduct of such transferred services in Northern Ireland, the argument goes, so why should Ulster MPs have a say in what happens in Great Britain? There is no particular logic in the situation, but a counter-argument is that the apparent anomaly is offset by the reduced representation at West-

minster. Possibly the best practical argument for full participation in Westminster affairs is that very many of the
decisions taken there affect Northern Ireland directly or
indirectly; in many fields, the government at Stormont
follows a 'step by step' policy. The Northern Ireland MP
suffers from one serious liability, in that he is denied experience of many of the constituency problems which are properly
brought to his Stormont counterpart; he may feel inhibited
about speaking on matters for which he has no responsibility
in his own constituency. Few, since 1920, have held office in
British governments or political parties; Sir Hugh O'Neill,
who became Lord Rathcavan, was chairman of the Conservatives' committee of backbenchers (the 1922 Committee) for a
period. Freedom from some constituency problems might seem
to indicate opportunity to specialise in important national
fields like defence and foreign affairs, but few MPs have taken
advantage of this; Mr H. Montgomery Hyde was a notable
advocate of social reforms, as in the law on capital punishment, but a consequence of his liberal views was that he lost
the Unionist nomination in North Belfast at the 1959 general
election. Possibly the calibre of Ulster MPs at Westminster
has fallen during the past fifty years; politicians ambitious
for ministerial office are more likely to seek seats at Stormont
than at Westminster. Certainly the preoccupations of Ulster
politics have tended to draw them out of the mainstream of
British politics; there is no clear distinction between national
and provincial politics, as there is in many countries which
practise a federal system of government.

Local government

Local government in Northern Ireland entered into a period
of uncertainty when, in March 1966, the minister of development (Mr Craig) initiated confidential talks with the principal
local government bodies on the reshaping of local government.
There were at that time two county borough councils (Belfast
and Londonderry), six county councils, ten borough councils,
twenty-four urban district councils and thirty-one rural
district councils, a total of seventy-three local authorities. In
essence, this was the structure established by the Local

Government Act (Ireland), 1898, which assumed a fairly clear distinction between urban and rural areas. It was not unlike the English pattern, though there were no parish councils, and it was better suited to a more rural and less mobile society than now exists; broadly speaking, an area enjoyed the standard of local services which it could afford. The 1898 Act tidied up local government, and placed it firmly on an elective basis; hitherto, grand juries had acted in the counties, and town commissioners had been common in urban areas. There continued to be boards of guardians, first introduced by the Poor Relief (Ireland) Act, 1838, which had acquired responsibility for public health as well as the relief of destitution. A number of their duties were taken over by the new councils but they continued to administer the poor law (through workhouses and outdoor relief) until 1948.

Under the traditional multi-tiered system of local government in Northern Ireland, the county councils and the county borough councils exercised the more important functions, and there was a continuing increase in these functions. Acting through statutory committees, the councils were education, health and welfare authorities. They were consequently responsible for ensuring efficient primary, secondary and further education; for maternity and child welfare services, health visiting, vaccination and immunisation, health education, school health services and the administration of the Food and Drug Acts; and for the welfare of the young, the aged and the physically or mentally handicapped. In addition, county councils exercised a number of powers within rural districts. They levied rates and were responsible for public works, including harbours, bridges and all but major roads; they were the planning authorities and had powers to prepare schemes to improve tourist amenities. The two county borough councils enjoyed the same powers, but also carried out the duties of urban district councils. In addition, a succession of local Acts added to their powers; thus Belfast was able to run its own transport service, to have its own fire service, and to have its water supplies administered by an independent local body of commissioners.

The powers of borough councils and urban district councils were broadly similar, but the former had power under the

Municipal Corporations (Ireland) Act, 1840, to confer on individuals the freedom of the borough. These councils had responsibility for water supplies, sewerage and sanitation; street lighting and cleansing; building houses for letting; and the planning and redevelopment of urban areas. They were responsible for the upkeep of streets and all but major roads, and for harbours. They were empowered to provide public parks and recreation grounds, art galleries and museums, swimming pools and libraries. They levied rates, but were required to hand over a proportion to county councils to meet the cost of county-wide services.

Finally, the rural district councils were primarily sanitary and housing authorities, acting in these fields much as the urban district councils did. They could also acquire some of the urban district councils' other powers by orders made under the Public Health and Local Government Acts. Their operations were financed by the county councils.

Local authorities in Northern Ireland have thus fulfilled much the same role as their counterparts in Great Britain, although it should be noted that they have not had the same responsibility for the so-called protective services : police, civil defence and (except in Belfast) fire services. Many local authority functions have been carried out by committees—in some cases, there was a statutory obligation to do so—which might include a proportion of non-elected members. Some authorities formed joint boards or committees for specific purposes, such as water and sewerage schemes. Authorities could also hand over functions; it was common for urban district councils to ask the county council to provide library services, and some drew on the services of the county planning officer on an informal basis. The Northern Ireland Housing Trust, a statutory body set up to supplement the local authority housing programme, has on occasions acted as a building agent for councils.

Local authorities have traditionally drawn their revenue from three sources : rates, government grants and receipts from services provided. The rateable value of land and buildings is determined according to their estimated annual letting value; this net annual value, or poor law valuation, is the profit an owner might expect to make by letting the property in the open market. Each year, the local authority fixes a rate —a specified sum per pound of valuation—and this determines the individual ratepayer's contribution. The poor law valuations are thus primarily a means of apportioning the rates burden. The present system dates back to the Valuation (Ireland) Act, 1852, which imposed a single method of assessment. The Valuations Acts Amendment Act (NI), 1932, provided for periodic reviews of rateable values, with the exception of agricultural land and buildings, which were to remain fixed. The first general revaluation came into effect on 1 April 1936, and the second on 1 April 1957. Under the second revaluation, dwelling houses were valued at 1939 levels while most other properties were valued at current levels; however, the Revaluation (Amendment and Consequential Provisions) Act (NI), 1957, did make some other reductions. There is, in addition, provision for an annual revision of valuation. In all cases, there is provision for appeal to the commissioner of valuation, a civil servant, and beyond him to the Lands Tribunal for Northern Ireland; the tribunal's decisions are final on questions of fact, but questions of law can be taken to the Court of Appeal.

Government grants to local authorities have tended to increase in recent years, and now account for more than half their revenue; education grants alone are higher than receipts from rates. This was not the case before World War II. In 1929, the Northern Ireland Government introduced derating, a measure adopted in Great Britain to help farmers and industrialists. Under the Local Government (Rating and Finance) Act (NI), agricultural land and buildings were exempted from rates, while industrial premises enjoyed a seventy-five per cent derating. (The latter proportion remained, as an aid to industrial development, even after industrial derating was abolished in England and Wales in 1963.) Other legislation has granted rates exemption to public properties, and to properties used for scientific and cultural purposes, and for charitable and religious purposes. The government provided derating grants to offset the loss of revenue.

Under the Local Government (Finance) Act (NI), 1948, these grants were replaced by a new grant called the general exchequer contribution. It was designed to encourage the development of local authority services, but the formula by which it was calculated proved unsatisfactory, and a new one was recommended in the 1957 report of the Committee on the Finances of Local Authorities (Cmd 369) under the chairmanship of Sir Roland Nugent. This not only provided full compensation for derating, but allowed for a system of weighting to provide additional finance, particularly for needy authorities. The formula was adopted in the Local Government (Finance) (No. 2) Act (NI), 1958, which provided for weighting according to road mileage and population within each local authority area, so helping sparsely populated areas which tended to have poor services. Since the general exchequer contribution was not designed to finance any specific service, it escaped the governmental scrutiny attached to those which were. However, the Act did give power to reduce the contribution where it appeared to the responsible ministry that a local authority was not maintaining a reasonable standard of efficiency or that its expenditure had been excessive.

As to grants for specific services, by far the largest government commitment is in the field of education, but substantial sums have been paid in grants for roads and health and welfare services. In each case, the independence of local authorities is limited by the need for ministry approval of particular schemes. Borrowing also requires ministry sanction, and a local government audit imposes a further curb; in the event of illegal expenditure, individual councillors can be surcharged. The government also imposes levies to finance some centralised services which in Great Britain are administered by local authorities; these include the youth employment service and the Northern Ireland Fire Authority.

The financing of education probably provides the main source of grievance among local authorities. The Education Act (NI), 1947, pooled annual expenditure on a number of items : the salaries of teachers other than in voluntary grammar schools, loan charges on loans raised between 1948 and 1968 for capital works, scholarships to pupils in grammar schools and school transport. The government's share of this expenditure was fixed at £2,335,000 ($5,604,000), roughly the initial liability under the Act, plus sixty-five per cent of the remainder. The thirty-five per cent borne by rates (offset, in part, by the general exchequer contribution) was allocated among authorities in proportion to their net annual valuation; thus the richer authorities tend to subsidise the poorer ones. Under the Education (Amendment) Act (NI), 1968, new loan charges ceased to be pooled and attracted an eighty per cent grant from 1 April 1968.

Other education grants to local authorities are more directly related to their expenditure. In the case of university scholarships, the Ministry of Education pays the amount by which their total expenditure exceeds £160,000 ($384,000); liability for the first £160,000 is distributed among the authorities in proportion to the total cost of university scholarships within each area. Grants of sixty-five per cent of approved expenditure are payable to local education authorities in a number of fields : administrative costs, maintenance of county schools, payments to managers of voluntary schools. Some items of expenditure attract an eighty per cent grant. The mounting cost of education has encouraged the argument that it should be removed altogether from local authorities, which have little control over expenditure when standards are set at a provincial or even national level. Local authorities have often tried to offset rising education charges by economising on local amenities.

Since 1967, an additional grant has been payable to reduce the domestic ratepayers' burden. Each year, the Ministry of Development fixes an amount per pound of valuation by which domestic rates are to be reduced, and pays a compensating grant to local authorities. The total grant rose from £600,000 ($1,440,000) in 1967-8 to £2,060,000 ($4,944,000) in 1970-1. This scheme followed a Westminster measure which ensured that rates relief went to the needy. The Northern Ireland Government chose not to introduce a means test, on the grounds that its administration would be costly, and the effect is that the wealthier ratepayers (those occupying dwellings with a high poor law valuation) receive most benefit.

On 20 December 1967, the government published a White Paper, *The Re-Shaping of Local Government: Statement of Aims* (Cmd 517), which proposed the establishment of between twelve and eighteen 'area councils' based on the historic

D

boroughs and towns of Northern Ireland. It was suggested that these councils could be responsible for such physical and environmental services as local roads and streets, action plans in town planning, housing, water, sewerage, sanitation, parks, playing fields, swimming pools, refuse or garbage disposal, implementing clean air legislation, car parks, noise control and prevention of water pollution; included also was the promotion of local entertainment and cultural activities. It was suggested that eventually there would be a one-tier system of local government, with the area councils as the sole elective bodies outside Belfast. However, it was proposed that a number of social services—education, libraries, personal health, school health, welfare and child care—should remain with the county councils for a substantial period, while their long-term future was being studied. The White Paper warned that area councils could not be allocated any responsibility for administering these social services.

The government set out three criteria in its statement of aims : efficiency, economy and effective representation of local aspirations. While discussions on the White Paper continued, there was an initial voluntary amalgamation of local authorities in county Fermanagh, where the powers of Enniskillen borough council and the three rural district councils were transferred to the county council on 2 June 1967. The pattern of local government was also altered as a result of the New Towns Act (NI), 1965, which provided for the creation of new towns and the expansion and development of existing ones. The first order made under the Act designated an area comprising the county Armagh boroughs of Lurgan and Portadown and the rural districts of Lurgan and Moira as the site for the new city of Craigavon; within this area, some 7,000 acres of land was distinguished for acquisition by the Ministry of Development, and most of this was eventually transferred to a development commission set up in October 1965. On 1 April 1967, the powers of Lurgan rural district council were transferred to the commission. It was originally estimated that the population of Craigavon would reach 100,000 by 1981. A development commission for the county Antrim towns of Antrim and Ballymena was similarly established on 8 September 1967, and the intention is to create an industrial complex of 100,000 people. Finally, the Unionist reform programme of 22 November 1968 provided for a development commission in Londonderry. On 2 April 1969, the powers of the county borough council and of Londonderry rural district council were transferred to the new commission.

On 2 July 1969, the government published a further White Paper, *The Re-Shaping of Local Government: Further Proposals* (Cmd 530). This delimited seventeen proposed area councils. These included Belfast, the area controlled by the Londonderry development commission, and (with minor alterations) the areas controlled by the Craigavon and Antrim-Ballymena commissions and by Fermanagh County Council. The suggestion that eventually there might be no place for county councils was repeated. The White Paper noted the report of the royal commission on local government in England, published on 11 June 1969, which recommended for most of England 'a series of essentially single-tier Councils, many of which will have a population running up to three quarters of a million or a million and most of which will enjoy a rate revenue greater than that of the whole of Northern Ireland'.

> The Government of Northern Ireland . . . in the Statement of Aims in 1967 foresaw the very tenable argument for one local authority for the whole of Northern Ireland, or indeed for doing away with local government entirely. They did not favour the idea of complete centralisation then nor do they now, because they prefer to find a system which enriches life in the various parts of the country; but they do envisage the need, on grounds of efficiency and economy, to base a number of services on larger units than the areas now proposed for local government, for the same logical reasons as have constrained the Royal Commission to recommend local units as big as—and even wealthier than—the whole of Northern Ireland. The essential difference may in the end prove to be the existence of an active and responsible level of Area Councils here, with an interesting and important range of functions; and this may turn out to be a valuable buttress to our democratic system.

In the White Paper, the government undertook to legislate for the appointment of an independent statutory commission to review wards and other electoral areas so as to bring them into line with present population and projected development, and to form the electoral constituencies of the councillors required for the area councils.

There was some criticism of the seventeen proposed areas, and then the future of local government was again thrown into the melting pot by the civil disorders during and after August 1969. The communique of 10 October announced an expanded housing programme, and said the Northern Ireland Government had

> reluctantly decided that local authorities are not geared—and cannot be geared—to handle such a task and that the best hope of success lies in the creation of a single-purpose, efficient and streamlined central housing authority (helped by the Development Commissions in their own areas) to tackle this most urgent problem.

It was recognised that the decision to centralise public housing —including the management of dwellings already built—had implications in such fields as water, sewerage, roads and recreational services, and in the staffing of councils which no longer had housing functions. With the future administrative structure of important social services already under review, the government took the decision to set up a review body to examine local government and advise on 'the most efficient distribution of the relevant functions'.

Not until 1969 did Northern Ireland adopt universal adult suffrage in local government and abolish plural voting. Probably the most effective slogan of the civil rights movement had been 'one man, one vote', and the reform programme of 22 November 1968 contained a commitment to 'review the franchise in the context of the organisation, financing and structure of the new local government bodies, and to abolish the company vote in local government'. Local government elections are held at three-yearly intervals, and it was the practice every third year to include in the annual register of parliamentary electors the names of those entitled to vote in council elections. To qualify as an elector, it was necessary to be a British subject at least twenty-one years old, and to have been born in Northern Ireland or to have resided continuously in the United Kingdom for the whole of the seven years preceding the qualifying date. It was further necessary to qualify as a resident occupier or general occupier. A resident occupier was the owner or tenant of a dwelling-house, and had to have lived there or elsewhere in Northern Ireland for the preceding three months; the occupier's husband or wife also received a vote. A general occupier was the owner or tenant of land or premises (not a dwelling-house) of an annual valuation not less than £10 ($24). Limited companies were entitled to appoint a nominee for every £10 of valuation, up to a maximum of six voters. However, while an elector might be able to cast a number of votes, he or she could only be registered under one qualification in any single local government electoral area. Some indication of the extent of disenfranchisement is given by the following table of electors in 1967 :

	Number of Electors
Stormont	933,724 (including 15,914 in the Queen's University constituency)
Westminster	909,841
Local government	694,483

In the reform programme of 22 November 1968, the government indicated

> its firm intention to complete a comprehensive reform and modernisation of the local government structure within a period of three years—that is, by the end of 1971—to review the franchise in the context of the organisation, financing and structure of the new local government bodies, and to abolish the company vote in local government.

However, under continuing pressure from the civil rights movement, the cabinet decided to commit itself to 'one man, one vote' before the new shape of local government was decided, and the Unionist parliamentary party endorsed the decision on 23 April 1969. The Minister of Agriculture, Major James Chichester-Clark, resigned from the government—'I question firstly whether this concession at this time will stop the activity in the streets, and secondly I fear that our supporters will lose all faith in the determination of the present Government'—but accepted the change of policy when he became prime minister a few days later, after the resignation of Capt O'Neill.

The new franchise was embodied in the Electoral Law (No. 2) Act (NI), 1969, which also postponed until 1971 the triennial elections due to be held in 1970. The Local Govern-

ment Act (NI), 1970, provided for a local government ward
boundaries commission, to make recommendations on the
number of wards and their boundaries within each administrative area. The government retained the right to determine
the number of administrative areas and their boundaries. However, on 11 December 1969 the Minister of Development, Mr
Brian Faulkner, announced the terms of reference of the local
government review body and added :

> It will not be any part of the review body's duty to attempt
> to define the new local authority areas nor to draw their
> boundaries. We wish them to be free to concentrate on prin-
> ciples and to base their advice on administrative considera-
> tions and the practical merits of the situation. If, when the
> report of the review body is received and considered, it is
> apparent that the pattern of local councils is such as to justify
> the drawing of new boundary lines by an impartial body of
> high standing, then in that event it is the intention of the
> Government to refer the matter to the parliamentary boun-
> dary commission for the Stormont constituencies and to
> request them to carry through the operation along the same
> procedures and methods as they employ in defining consti-
> tuencies.

The chairman of the review body was Mr Patrick Macrory,
and the six-man body contained an equal number of Protestants and Catholics. Its report (Cmd 546) was published on 25
June 1970, and it divided the functions under review
into two broad categories : regional functions which
required large units for administration, and district services
which could be efficiently administered in small units. The
report's main recommendation was that Stormont should be
responsible for the regional services, and that not more than
twenty-six district councils should administer the remainder
of the services.

The regional functions were defined as : education; public
libraries; personal health, welfare and child care; planning;
roads and traffic management; motor taxation; housing; water
and major sewerage systems; food composition, standards and
labelling; tourism; electoral arrangements; criminal injuries
compensation; gas; electricity; transport; major harbours; fire.
It was recommended that each of these be directly assigned to
appropriate ministries, with the exception of trading under-

takings (gas, electricity, municipal transport in Belfast, and major harbours) and the fire service (divided between the Northern Ireland Fire Authority, established in 1950, and Belfast Corporation). The review body rejected the idea of autonomous boards as unsuitable except for a very limited range of technical or operational functions.

The functions of the elected district councils, each based on a main town or city, were defined as : environmental health; cleansing; urban drainage; minor harbours; minor sewerage; public conveniences; cemeteries and crematoria; bylaw control of buildings; recreation; entertainment and culture; protective services; regulatory services; bylaws; markets and abattoirs; civic improvement schemes. It was suggested that district councils should be free to spend the product of a 2½p (6c) rate on any purpose not otherwise authorised by statute. Small community groups were to be encouraged, with provision for financial assistance for approved purposes. The review body envisaged that the rates struck each year should be in two parts : a regional portion imposed uniformly throughout Northern Ireland, and a district portion struck independently by each district council.

The review body came down strongly in favour of the 'representative principle'; in some quarters, it had been felt that non-elective bodies offered a better prospect of ensuring that the Catholic minority played a real part in public life and decision-taking. However, the members of the review body said they had 'refused throughout to adopt doctrinaire attitudes on the merits or demerits of elected local councils, appointed boards, centralisation and other vexed issues, nor have we let ourselves be drawn into political argument or debate on the past record of local government in Northern Ireland'. One consequence of the proposals, which were to be widely debated before the government would reach a decision on them, was a further postponement of local government elections. Another possible consequence, discussed briefly in the report, was the possible need for a larger House of Commons and the establishment of select committees to deal with the regional services. The report also envisaged the delegation of responsibilities to area boards in the case of education, the personal health and social services, and child care.

For this purpose, Northern Ireland could be divided into four areas; the boards within each area would be appointed by the responsible minister and would be clearly the ministry's agent, and the membership would represent the community served and include a proportion of district councillors.

Proportional representation in council elections was introduced by the Local Government (Ireland) Act, 1919. It had been included in the unimplemented 1914 Act, and Nicholas Mansergh described its working in *The Government of Northern Ireland:*

> The elections for the urban and municipal councils were held early in 1920; the County Council elections in the summer of the same year. The results showed that P.R. was definitely favourable to minority representation both in North and South. They also served to dispel the illusion that the north-eastern counties of Ulster were entirely Unionist. Public interest centred largely upon a dramatic contest which decided the majority party in the Tyrone County Council election. In this county the Nationalists had gained a recent but slight numerical advantage. Under P.R. the party, composed of constitutional Nationalists and Sinn Fein working in co-operation, secured the majority to which their voting strength entitled them. The new electoral system was received with favour by all parties other than the Ulster Unionists.

The Unionist government proceeded to abolish proportional representation, and after the delayed granting of royal assent to the Local Government Bill (NI), 1922, drew local government electoral boundaries in such a way that a number of councils passed under Unionist control. With the abolition of proportional representation, the number of contested seats fell.

The judiciary

The administration of justice in Northern Ireland is broadly similar to the system prevailing in England and Wales. Under section 38 of the 1920 Act, the Supreme Court of Judicature in Ireland ceased to exist, and was replaced by the Supreme Court of Judicature of Northern Ireland. There are two divisions of the court. The High Court initially consisted of the lord chief justice, who is its president, and two puisne judges; section 1 of the Administration of Justice Act, 1968, made provision for the appointment of two additional judges. The Court of Appeal consists of the lord chief justice, as president, and two lord justices of appeal. Both courts sit in the Royal Courts of Justice in Belfast. The High Court has two divisions. The Queen's Bench Division deals with all criminal matters, in addition to such matters as applications for writs of habeas corpus and orders of mandamus or certiorari, and with common law proceedings concerning such matters as breach of contract and damages. The division also embraces cases which in England would be dealt with in the Probate, Divorce and Admiralty Division. There is also a Chancery Division, dealing with such matters as the administration of trusts, title to land and the administration of joint stock companies. The Court of Appeal has power to review High Court decisions, and in some instances the decisions of lower courts. An appeal from the Court of Appeal is made to the House of Lords. Not every judgement can be questioned in this way, but there is an absolute right of appeal when the validity of Stormont legislation is in question. The Administration of Justice Act, 1960, provided for an appeal to the Lords against a Court of Appeal judgement in a criminal matter on a case stated by a county court or magistrate's court. However, it has to be certified that a point of law of general public importance is involved.

A Court of Criminal Appeal was established by the Criminal Appeal (Northern Ireland) Act, 1930, and consists of all the judges of the Supreme Court. It normally sits in Belfast, and persons convicted on indictment can appeal to it on a point of law or (with leave of the court) on a question of fact, or against sentence. Judges of the High Court also receive commissions to hold assizes in each county town at stated times of the year. These assizes are held in spring and autumn, and deal with both criminal and civil cases. There is also a winter assize, dealing with criminal cases, which covers the whole of Northern Ireland except Belfast. There is no assize court for Belfast, but instead a Supreme Court judge presides over the City Commission four times a year. All matters relating to the Supreme Court of Judicature and the Court of Criminal Appeal are reserved matters under the jurisdiction of Westminister. On occasions, a lord justice sits in the High Court to ease the pressure of work, and a High Court judge can also be asked to sit in the Court of Appeal. The lord chief justice has personal jurisdiction over the administration of the property and income of persons of unsound mind, the wardship of minors (both jurisdictions formerly exercised by the lord chancellor of Ireland), and the adoption of children under the Adoption of Children Act (NI), 1950.

In 1970, a committee under the chairmanship of the Lord Chief Justice, Lord MacDermott, recommended a number of changes in the Supreme Court. Its report (UK Cmd 4292) called for abolition of the existing divisions of the High Court, and for the transfer of the business of the Court of Criminal Appeal to the Court of Appeal. It recommended also that appeals in habeas corpus cases should be first to the Court of Appeal and then, with leave, to the House of Lords rather than directly to the Lords. The report considered problems arising from the fact that, while the Supreme Court is a reserved matter, it has to deal with legislation from Stormont. Three possible solutions are considered : a wide enabling measure to be passed by Westminster, de-reservation of the Supreme Court, and enablement through repeal of limiting sections of the 1920 Act except for 'such essential subject-matters as ought to be kept within the exclusive power of Westminster'. The argument against de-reservation was that Northern Ireland is

> a small area where controversy has abounded among a small and hitherto divided community. We believe that confidence in the administration of justice at the highest level has been and will be best promoted and maintained by keeping the superior courts entirely outside the realm of local political contention.

The committee pointed to the advantage of having the ultimate oversight of the lord chancellor in London, who is both head of the judiciary and a member of the British Government. In practice, a number of enabling measures have been required to clarify, rather than to extend, the powers of the Northern Ireland Parliament in relation to the Supreme Court. The most important of these measures are the Northern Ireland (Miscellaneous Provisions) Acts, 1928 and

1932, and the Northern Ireland Act, 1962. Section 1(1) of the 1932 Act, for example, deals with the restrictiveness of section 47 of the 1920 Act, which states that 'All matters relating to the Supreme Court of Northern Ireland shall be reserved matters'. The 1932 Act states that this reservation 'shall not be construed as precluding the Parliament of Northern Ireland from enacting, for the purpose of a branch of the law the general subject-matter of which is within the powers of that Parliament, provisions conferring jurisdiction on the Supreme Court, the High Court, or a court of assize'. There is some doubt, however, about Stormont's powers to withdraw jurisdiction from the Supreme Court, even when it has originally been conferred by local legislation.

The remaining courts are wholly under the jurisdiction of the Northern Ireland Parliament. These include the county courts, the magistrates' courts and the coroners' courts. There are five county court judges. One is recorder of Belfast, and acts also for county Antrim; another is recorder of Londonderry, and acts also for the surrounding county; one judge is responsible for both Armagh and Fermanagh. Originally, county court judges also presided over courts of quarter sessions, held in each quarter of the year, with much the same jurisdiction in criminal matters as assize courts; these courts also dealt with appeals from the magistrates' courts, appeals on such matters as valuation and liquor licensing, and questions concerning lists of jurors and the registration of voters. Under the County Courts Act (NI), 1959, all these functions were embraced by the county courts. The latter sit at least four times annually in each county court division and (except for grave offences) the decision on whether an accused man is returned for trial at a county or assize court is likely to depend on which offers the speediest trial. The county courts have what is known as a 'civil bill' jurisdiction to deal with civil actions in which the amount claimed or the value of the articles claimed does not exceed £300 ($720). Exceptions are libel and slander, for which the damages claimed must not exceed £50 ($120); by contrast, cases can be remitted from the High Court, and in these the £300 limit does not apply. Divorce is outside the jurisdiction of the county courts, as are actions involving the title to any toll, market, fair or franchise.

Jurisdiction extends to actions for the recovery of land or involving the title to land where the valuation does not exceed £75 ($180). In various other civil actions, jurisdiction is limited to a sum not exceeding £1,000 ($2,400). County courts are responsible for criminal injury cases and workmen's compensation cases. Appeals may be made to the assize judge and thereafter, with leave and on questions of law, to the Court of Appeal.

The magistrates' courts, known also as courts of summary jurisdiction or petty sessions, deal with minor criminal or quasi-criminal cases and minor civil disputes such as trespass and the recovery of small debts. There are more than seventy petty sessions districts, in which courts are held at regular intervals—daily in Belfast—with a salaried resident magistrate presiding. In Ireland, salaried magistrates were introduced under the Constabulary (Ireland) Act, 1836, in consequence of disorders in the country and the fact that the prevalence of absentee landlords made it difficult to find justices of the peace of English calibre. Originally, it was the practice to have lay justices sitting with the resident magistrates, but following criticism of their conduct the Summary Jurisdiction and Criminal Justice Act (NI), 1935, removed almost all their judicial functions. The resident magistrate now normally sits alone; exceptions include special crimes courts, at which two magistrates preside, and juvenile courts, where the magistrate is accompanied by two lay members (one of whom must be a woman).

Broadly speaking, the judicial systems of Northern Ireland and of England and Wales are similar. The legal profession is similarly divided into barristers and solicitors; only barristers can be heard in the superior courts, and judges are chosen from their ranks. The Inn of Court of Northern Ireland was formed in 1926, and regulates admissions to the bar. Solicitors are supervised by the Incorporated Law Society of Northern Ireland, established by royal charter in 1922. The impartiality of the judiciary has sometimes been challenged, but this reflects Northern Ireland's politico-religious divisions and no persuasive evidence has been adduced. There is, however, a preponderance of Protestant appointees to the bench. This is not surprising, when political service is commonly rewarded by a judicial appointment, and it has always been the practice to have one or more Catholics in the Supreme Court, the county courts and the magistracy; a Catholic, Sir Denis Henry, became Northern Ireland's first lord chief justice.

3

Political Parties

In *The Government of Northern Ireland*, Nicholas Mansergh wrote :

> Parties in Ulster emphasize traditional religious and racial antagonisms in order to exact a rigid loyalty from their supporters. They intensify a sectarian bitterness which civilized opinion deplores; and in so doing they force the judgment of the electors into the service of their prejudices . . . . The main criticism, therefore, that one would direct against the operation of the party system in Northern Ireland is not that it fails to permit of nice shades of distinction in public opinion—for that were outside its function— nor yet that it fosters a bellicose spirit, though indeed the pugnacity of the respective parties might, with advantage, be restrained—but that it subordinates every vital issue, whether of social or economic policy, to the dead hand of sectarian strife.

This 1936 judgement has lost some of its validity, but the experiences of the past decade have shown how difficult it is to break away from traditional sectarianism. The governing Unionist Party fought the Stormont general election of 24 February 1969 on a manifesto which it described as a declaration of principle as well as a statement of policy :

> The Ulster Unionist Party believes in an Ulster in which the obligations and rights of all citizens will be fully recognised. It expects of all citizens that loyalty towards the State which is due when the institutions of that State have the expressed support of a clear majority. It seeks from every individual a proper sense of responsibility and wholehearted participation in the life of the State. The Party acknowledges and proclaims the right of all citizens to equal treatment

under the law, to full equality in the enjoyment of health, education and other social benefits and to the protection of authority against every kind of injustice. . . . The Party will work to heal those divisions in our community which have so far prevented Northern Ireland from fulfilling its best hopes.

In fact, the party went into the election deeply divided, and these internal divisions led soon afterwards to the resignation of the Prime Minister, Capt Terence O'Neill. His successor, Major James Chichester-Clark, also found it difficult to maintain unity and discipline within the party, and to hold on to traditional electoral support from Northern Ireland Protestants. Nonetheless, the Unionists remained in power as they had done since 1921.

The Ulster Unionist Council was formed in March 1905, bringing together a number of organisations dedicated to preserving the union with Great Britain—and perhaps foreshadowing the subsequent willingness to yield the other Irish provinces (and, as it turned out, three Ulster counties) to the insistent demands of Irish nationalism. The union had been the subject of political controversy throughout the nineteenth century, but it was the conversion of William Ewart Gladstone to the home rule cause in 1885 that opened up a real prospect of Irish independence. The Liberal leader had earlier declared that his mission was to pacify Ireland, and his first abortive Home Rule Bill was introduced soon after he became prime minister in 1886. There were at this time more than eighty Irish Nationalists in the British House of Commons, under the leadership of Charles Stewart Parnell, while the Ulster Unionists under Edward Saunderson were very much a party within the Conservative Party. Col Saunderson joined the Orange Order in 1882, and while Westminster was debating Gladstone's second Home Rule Bill in 1893 he helped to establish the Ulster Defence Union for the purpose of resisting home rule by force. Initially, at least, Saunderson opposed home rule for any part of Ireland. The Ulster Unionist Council had links with the Irish Unionist Alliance, whose headquarters was in Dublin, and a concerted effort was made to present unionism's case to the British public. However, the major task was to provide a central policy-making body in

Ulster, and to develop an organisation capable of being converted into a military force.

At first, there were two hundred members of the council, which operated through an executive committee. One hundred members represented local Unionist associations, fifty represented the Orange Order and fifty the Ulster MPs. These numbers steadily expanded, and the council's 1970 yearbook gave the membership as :

(a) 306 nominated by the affiliated Divisional Associations in accordance with the numbers set forth in the Schedule;
(b) 234 nominated by the Women's Associations affiliated to the Ulster Women's Unionist Council;
(c) 122 nominated by the County Grand Lodges of the Loyal Orange Institution of Ireland;
(d) 20 nominated by the Ulster Unionist Labour Association;
(e) 20 nominated by the Ulster Women's Unionist Council;
(f) 12 nominated by the Ulster Reform Club Political Council;
(g) 12 nominated by the Queen's University Unionist Voters' Association;
(h) 6 nominated by the Apprentice Boys of Derry;
(i) 6 nominated by the Willowfield Unionist Club;
(j) 10 nominated by the Association of Loyal Orange Women of Ireland;
(k) 12 nominated by the Unionist Society;
(l) the Northern Irish Peers, the Members representing Ulster Constituencies in the Imperial House of Commons at Westminster and the Members of the Senate and of the House of Commons of the Parliament of Northern Ireland, who, in the opinion of the Standing Committee hereinafter referred to, are members of the Unionist Party;
(m) the wives of such Peers, Senators and Members of Parliament if they so desire;
(n) also distinguished persons who may from time to time be co-opted by the Council, but the number of such co-opted members shall not exceed 120 at any one time.

In addition, divisional associations which had an active Young Unionist association attached could choose an extra delegate from the latter body. Thus, in 1970, the Ulster Unionist Council had close to 1,000 members. However, the council customarily meets only once a year, and its business is conducted by a standing committee which meets four times a year. The standing committee is also an unwieldy body, with more than 300 members; in representation, it is really a scaled-down version of the council, except that Unionist peers, senators and all MPs belong to it. The standing committee elects annually an executive committee, which meets monthly. It is required, in choosing the thirty-six elected members, that 'A territorial basis of membership shall be maintained', and there is a specific provision for two representatives each from the Orange Order, the Young Unionists and Unionist Labour. A number of office-bearers of the council and the standing committee are ex-officio members, as are the leader of the party (by convention, the leader of the parliamentary party), the chief whip, a Westminster MP nominated by the leader, and two representatives of the Ulster Women's Unionist Council.

After Col Saunderson's death in 1906, the Unionist MPs were briefly led by Walter Long, a former chief secretary for Ireland and founder of the Union Defence League. In 1910, he was succeeded by Sir Edward Carson, a former solicitor-general who represented the University of Dublin. Carson had little knowledge of Ulster, but regarded the province as a weapon he could use to maintain the union with Great Britain in its entirety. Initially, Carson's role was a parliamentary one. However, the passing of the Parliament Act in August 1911—curbing the power of the House of Lords to defeat or delay legislation—opened the way to a home rule Act. Carson was now the leader of a popular movement which was prepared to use force to resist the implementation of a parliamentary decision. On 23 September 1911, he told a gathering of thousands of Ulster Protestants on the outskirts of Belfast that 'We will yet defeat the most nefarious conspiracy that has ever been hatched against a free people'. Carson said they must be prepared 'the morning Home Rule passes, ourselves to become responsible for the government of the protestant province of Ulster'. Ulster unionism was able to command the support of the Conservatives, even for its more extreme actions. On 9 April 1912, Bonar Law, the Conservative leader, told more than 100,000 unionists in Belfast that 'when the crisis is over men will say to you in words not unlike those used by Pitt—you have saved yourself by your exertions, and you will save the Empire by your example'. In July 1912, he warned:

E

'I can imagine no length of resistance to which Ulster will go, in which I shall not be ready to support them, and in which they will not be supported by the overwhelming majority of the British people'.

Of the Ulster Protestants' fervour there was no doubt. On 28 September 1912, thousands signed 'Ulster's solemn league and covenant', a document inspired by the Scottish covenant of 1580; eventually, there were almost half a million signatures, some of them in blood.

> Being convinced in our consciences that Home Rule would be disastrous to the material well-being of Ulster as well as of the whole of Ireland, subversive of our civil and religious freedom, destructive of our citizenship and perilous to the unity of the Empire, we, whose names are underwritten, men of Ulster, loyal subjects of His Gracious Majesty King George V, humbly relying on the God whom our fathers in days of stress and trial confidently trusted, do hereby pledge ourselves in solemn Covenant throughout this our time of threatened calamity to stand by one another in defending for ourselves and our children our cherished position of equal citizenship in the United Kingdom and in using all means which may be found necessary to defeat the present conspiracy to set up a Home Rule Parliament in Ireland. And in the event of such a Parliament being forced upon us we further solemnly and mutually pledge ourselves to refuse to recognise its authority.

Unionism, then as now, appeared an inextricable mixture of religion and politics. Church leaders were closely associated with the unionist cause; in 1892, a vast convention held in Belfast to oppose Gladstone's second Home Rule Bill was led in prayer by the Church of Ireland primate of all Ireland and the moderator of the Presbyterian general assembly.

However, while the Ulster unionists were prepared to defend their place in the United Kingdom—even to the point of a successful gun-running operation in April 1914, to arm the Ulster Volunteer Force which had been set up by the Ulster Unionist Council the previous year—they were also prepared to reach a compromise. Not only were they prepared to abandon the unionists of the three other provinces, but they were prepared to cede three Ulster counties. The proportions of Protestants and Catholics revealed by the 1911 census illustrate the unionist dilemma.

	Protestants	Catholics
	%	%
Antrim	79.5	20.5
Down	68.4	31.6
Armagh	54.7	45.3
Londonderry	54.2	45.8
Tyrone	44.6	55.4
Fermanagh	43.8	56.2
Monaghan	25.3	74.7
Donegal	21.1	78.9
Cavan	18.5	81.5

Had Cavan, Donegal and Monaghan become part of Northern Ireland, the Protestant majority would have been about 200,000. Within the six counties, it was almost twice as high, the Protestants forming about two-thirds of the population. But the unionists were determined to hold on to two counties, Fermanagh and Tyrone, in which Protestants were in a minority; hence the Northern Ireland Government's unwillingness to nominate a member of the boundary commission set up under the 1921 treaty.

All this was a narrower unionism than Carson embraced, and in retrospect the Dublin barrister appears more a figurehead and spokesman than shaper of events. Immediately after the demonstration of 23 September 1911, moves were made to provide for a provisional government of Ulster; a five-man commission was appointed to work out a constitution, with 'due regard to the interests of loyalists in other parts of Ireland'. As an orator, Carson could command the devotion of Ulster's Protestant masses—masses who at different times have responded to orators able to play on their fears—and at the same time articulate their feelings to the British public. But, as Hugh Shearman wrote in *Not an Inch*:

> The blending of the views of Sir Edward Carson with those of the blunt, tongue-tied Ulstermen who had chosen him as their leader was not immediate. It was by a gradual process that the great lawyer and parliamentarian became the pupil and the convert of the men who held to a doctrine of frank, unconstitutional resistance and an ultimate appeal to the persuasive force of blood and iron. It was because he was willing to become the pupil and convert of these men that he remained their leader.

In *The Making of Modern Ireland 1603-1923*, J. C. Beckett pointed out that

> Carson, the Dublin lawyer, was their spokesman in Britain and their popular hero at home; but the man who most fully embodied their fears, their prejudices, their arrogance, their courage and their stubborn self-regard was one of themselves —James Craig, member for East Down, and a typical representative of the wealthy middle class that controlled the economic and political life of the province.

It was Craig who became Northern Ireland's first prime minister, for Carson had by then given up the leadership. Carson was the architect of partition—in 1913, he put forward an amendment to the home rule Bill calling for the exclusion of the nine Ulster counties—but his success lay in implementing the ideas of Craig rather than his own.

Nicholas Mansergh summed up Craig's administration in *The Government of Northern Ireland* :

> In its extreme opposition to compromise, in the well-nigh religious fervour of its Unionism, in its thinly disguised contempt for the niceties of constitutional government, it reflected Carson's own political creed. And inasmuch as the violent political atmosphere of pre-War years has exercised a decisive formative influence on the character of present-day Ulster Unionism, so the task of establishing a genuinely popular democratic system of government in the North has proved impossible of fulfilment.

The character of unionism was established by its early struggles, and has been little modified by the passing years. There is a defensive element, a siege mentality expressed in such negative slogans as 'No surrender' and 'Not an inch'. This is particularly marked in the three western counties of Fermanagh, Tyrone and Londonderry, perhaps reflecting the fact that there is a concentration of Protestant settlement along the western border with areas of Catholic dominance immediately to the east. It is marked also in those Protestant working-class districts of Belfast which abut on the Catholic 'ghetto' of west Belfast, possibly dating back to the influx of workers during the industrial revolution of the nineteenth century. Ronald McNeill, later Lord Cushendun, wrote in *Ulster's Stand for Union* of 'descendants of the Plantation men who had been deliberately sent to Ireland with a commission of the first sovereign of a United Britain to uphold British interest, British honour, and the reformed Faith'. However, there was always a strong and simple element of sectarianism, encouraged by some clergy and finding expression in sporadic rioting in the city.

There has always been a strong element of fear in unionism. There is fear of Roman Catholicism, fear of coming under an Irish parliament dominated by Catholics. Unionist politicians have not hesitated to encourage and play on these fears, as a means of maintaining the solidarity of the Protestant vote and of concentrating political struggles on a single issue; provided that the electorate divided according to religious beliefs, success seemed assured. Inevitably, though, there has been an accompanying fear of betrayal; Ulster has its own word for traitor, 'Lundy', recalling a seventeenth-century governor of Londonderry who was prepared to yield the city to Catholic James II. There was a sense of betrayal in 1916, when men of the Ulster Volunteer Force—who had retained their identity as a British army division—suffered heavy casualties through inadequate support at the Battle of the Somme.

Distrust of the Liberal Party has, in recent years, tended to be transferred to the British Labour Party; it has been fostered for a political objective, the election of Unionist MPs who accept the Conservative whip at Westminster. Moreover, Northern Protestants are capable of distrusting their own leaders. The early leaders abandoned three Ulster counties—not to mention three other provinces—and accepted a form of home rule in 1921. Under economic pressure, they yielded much of Northern Ireland's financial independence. In 1965, Capt O'Neill seemed to abandon traditional unionism by receiving the Prime Minister of the Republic of Ireland, Mr Sean Lemass, at Stormont. In 1969, following serious civil disorders, Major Chichester-Clark's administration seemed to be accepting the dictates of the British Government in matters nominally within Stormont's jurisdiction. Unionism has always had an uncompromising appearance, but the reality has been somewhat different, and this has always left the governing party vulnerable to criticism from Protestant extremists.

Traditionally, the Unionist Party's answer has been to outdo the extremists. In 1931, the Ulster Protestant League was formed, an anti-Catholic organisation whose policy was 'Neither to talk nor walk with, neither to buy nor sell, borrow nor lend, take nor give, or to have any dealings at all with them, nor for employers to employ them, nor employees to work with them'. The following year, Lord Craigavon assured an Orange demonstration that 'Ours is a Protestant government and I am an Orangeman', and in 1934 told the Commons :

> I am very proud indeed to be Grand Master of the Orange Institution of the loyal County of Down. I have filled that office for many years and I prize that far more than I do being Prime Minister. I have always said I am an Orangeman first and a politician and a Member of this Parliament afterwards . . . all I boast is that we are a Protestant Parliament and a Protestant State.

In 1933, Sir Basil Brooke told an Orange demonstration : 'Many in the audience employ Catholics, but I have not one about my place. Catholics are out to destroy Ulster with all their might and power. They want to nullify the Protestant vote, take all they can out of Ulster and then see it go to hell'. The following year, he enlarged on this statement by saying :

> I recommend those people who are loyalists not to employ Roman Catholics, ninety-nine per cent of whom are disloyal . . . usually there are plenty of good men and women available and the employers don't bother to employ them. You are disfranchising yourselves in that way. You people who are employers have the ball at your feet. If you don't act properly now, before we know where we are we shall find ourselves in the minority instead of the majority.

In 1932, Protestants in the Shankill Road area of Belfast had rioted in support of unemployed Catholics, whom police had baton-charged in nearby Falls Road. In 1935, a dozen people were killed when riots in the city took their traditional sectarian form.

The constitution of the Ulster Unionist Council defines its objectives in these words :

The objects of the Council shall be to maintain Northern Ireland as an integral part of the United Kingdom; to uphold and defend the Constitution and Parliament of Northern Ireland; to bring together all Unionist Associations in Northern Ireland, with a view to consistent and continuous political action; to act as a link between Ulster Unionists and their Parliamentary representatives; and to be the medium of expressing Ulster Unionist opinion, as current events may from time to time require, and generally to promote the interests of Unionism.

The words of Sir Basil Brooke, then minister of agriculture and later prime minister, are not wholly representative of unionist thinking—segregation in employment is far from absolute, particularly in larger concerns—but the determination of Protestants not to be outvoted by Catholics has been a critical element in unionism. In practice, this has meant at different levels a policy of restricting Catholics' opportunities —notably in employment and housing—so that population ratios and consequently political power remain fairly constant. The prospect of converting substantial numbers of Catholics to the unionist cause has not been taken seriously by many Unionist politicians until comparatively recently. Moreover, whilst it seemed that the development of the British welfare state since World War II had made a united Ireland less attractive to many Catholics—a growing Catholic middle class was on fairly good terms with its Protestant counterpart— the Unionist Party itself made no effort to recruit Catholic members. Many of its active members were openly anti-Catholic and unwilling to believe that a Catholic could be trusted when he said he supported the union with Great Britain. Catholics have consequently been reluctant to attempt to join the party, and have been particularly deterred by the party's continued link with the Orange Order.

In December 1959, the question of Catholic membership of the party was raised at a Young Unionist political school at Portstewart, county Londonderry. In a speech, Sir Clarence Graham, chairman of the standing committee of the Ulster Unionist Council, said he did not rule out the possibility that the day might come when many members of the Nationalist Party would wish to join the Unionist Party. Answering a question, he said he saw no reason why a Catholic should not be selected as a Unionist parliamentary candidate. Mr Brian Maginess, the Attorney-General, made a speech in which he called for greater toleration and co-operation between all sections of the community. In the ensuing and rather confused controversy, both men were widely criticised in Unionist circles, much of the criticism being based on an assumption that 'Roman Catholic' and 'nationalist' were necessarily synonymous. However, the Unionist executive committee issued a statement which could be interpreted as tacit support for their views. It pointed out that

> . . . the policy and aims of the Unionist Party remain unchanged and are as laid down by Edward Carson and James Craig, namely:
> (1) To maintain the constitutional position of Northern Ireland as an integral part of the United Kingdom and to defend the principles of civil and religious liberty;
> (2) To improve social standards and to expand industry and agriculture; and
> (3) To welcome to our ranks only those who unconditionally support these ideals.

Within a few days, the grand master of the Grand Orange Lodge of Ireland, Sir George Clark, made a speech asserting that under no circumstances would the suggestion that Catholics could be admitted to membership of the party be countenanced or accepted by the Orange Order. He said:

> I would draw your attention to the words 'civil and religious liberty'. This liberty, as we know it, is the liberty of the Protestant religion . . . In view of this, it is difficult to see how a Roman Catholic, with the vast differences in our religious outlook, could be either acceptable within the Unionist Party as a member or, for that matter, bring himself unconditionally to support its ideals. Further to this, an orangeman is pledged to resist by all lawful means the ascendancy of the Church of Rome, abstaining from uncharitable words, actions and sentiments towards his Roman Catholic brethren.

He added that it was possible that many Catholics might wish 'to remain within the Commonwealth', and that the way was open to them to support the Unionist Party through the ballot box. Sir George's views were not contradicted by the party, and the controversy petered out after the Prime Minister, Lord Brookeborough, said the Portstewart speeches had been quite unnecessary and that those concerned were 'charging at windmills and beating their heads against a wall about an issue which did not exist and which probably will not arise'.

In fact, there has always been a small number of Catholics within the Unionist Party—one prominent figure was a convert to Catholicism—but it was not until Capt O'Neill's premiership that any significant increase in this number seemed possible. However, power to accept or reject new applicants rested with local associations, and many of these would probably take the view that it is safer to exclude Catholics than risk what Lord Brookeborough called in 1959 'upsetting the loyalty of the people'. It was implicit in O'Neill's attempts to bridge the religious divisions in Northern Ireland that the Unionist Party should look for Catholic recruits, but little was done publicly and probably little was achieved. Many members of the party remained anti-Catholic in their attitudes, and it appeared to many Catholics that O'Neill's 'bridge-building' stemmed less from a new appreciation of the Catholic community as a whole than from the purely political motive of finding a new means to offset the higher Catholic birth-rate. This view received some substantiation from some of O'Neill's comments following his resignation in 1969, and particularly from a radio interview in which he said :

The basic fear of the Protestants in Northern Ireland is that they will be outbred by the Roman Catholics. It is as simple as that. It is frightfully hard to explain to a Protestant that if you give Roman Catholics a good job and a good house they will live like Protestants, because they will see neighbours with cars and television sets. They will refuse to have eighteen children. But if the Roman Catholic is jobless and lives in a most ghastly hovel, he will rear eighteen children on national assistance. It is impossible to explain this to a militant Protestant, because he is so keen to deny civil rights to his Roman Catholic neighbours. He cannot understand, in fact, that if you treat Roman Catholics with due consideration and kindness they will live like Protestants in spite of the authoritative nature of their church.

O'Neill subsequently said that he had not intended to offend Catholics, and added : 'If there was one paramount theme of my premiership, it was my attempt to improve community relations and to place the relationship between the majority and the minority on a basis of mutual respect'. His successor, Major James Chichester-Clark, has since given an assurance that Catholics are welcome in the Unionist Party, and said in November 1969 :

> I want to make it very clear indeed that, in the name of the party, I welcome those Roman Catholics who wish to be associated with unionism and support its principles—not just as voters, but as active party members with, of course, an equal right with all other party members to be considered for party office and all that flows from it.

Criticism of the structure of the Unionist Party has grown in recent years. This has centred on such matters as the composition of the Ulster Unionist Council, the lack of central discipline imposed by party headquarters on individual associations, the quality of candidates selected by local associations, and lack of uniformity in the rules of different associations. In December 1969, the Unionist standing committee recommended that only those who lived within a parliamentary constituency could vote at meetings of a divisional association, and only those living within a particular polling district could vote at a branch meeting; similarly, it was recommended that only those who were on the current register of electors for a division and who were pledged to accept fully the decision of the selection committee would have the right to vote for parliamentary and local candidates. The recommendation had a dual purpose : to meet the challenge of right-wing infiltration of constituency associations, whereby a small but determined group might have a wide influence on the selection of candidates, and to ensure that party members disappointed by the outcome of selection procedures did not (as happened at the 1969 election) lend support to other candidates. However, the recommendation was not binding on local associations, and some refused to adopt it. In April 1970, Major Chichester-Clark announced at the annual conference of the Ulster Unionist Council that he proposed to set up a small committee to examine 'the rules and the structure of the party to see how they match up to four vital criteria—democracy, efficiency, consistency and loyalty'.

The Unionist Party has held power in Northern Ireland since 1921, when it won forty of the fifty-two Commons seats. Its majority has always been comfortable, though in 1970 the expulsion of five members of the parliamentary party and the subsequent loss of two by-elections reduced the number of MPs receiving the Unionist whip to twenty-eight. A number of other MPs, including those expelled and the Protestant Unionist victors of the by-elections, were committed to supporting the constitutional link with Great Britain. In 1967, a survey carried out by National Opinion Polls Limited for the *Belfast Telegraph* posed the question : 'If there were an election for Stormont tomorrow, which party would you be most likely to support?' The response, classified by religion, indicated the Unionist Party's command of the Protestant vote.

	All	Church of Ireland	Presbyterian	Roman Catholic	Others
	%	%	%	%	%
Unionist	53	83	80	4	74
Nationalist	11	—	*	30	1
Labour	19	11	13	33	11
Republican Labour	2	—	—	6	—
Liberal	6	2	3	12	1
National Democrat	*	—	—	1	—
Other parties	*	*	1	—	—
None/don't know/refused	9	4	3	14	13

(* less than 0.5 per cent.)

Of all the opposition parties, Labour has been the most consistent in depriving the Unionists of an appreciable proportion of the Protestant vote. However, the Unionists have proved vulnerable at different times to other challenges. In 1925, a member of the government lost his seat to a representative of the 'unbought tenants', and in 1929 election there were 'local option' candidates who sought changes in the liquor licensing laws. In 1938, Progressive Unionists pressed for a more vigorous economic policy. From time to time,

Independent Unionists have sat at Stormont, usually representing an uncompromising Protestantism in their constituencies.

Possibly the most serious challenge which has emerged is the Protestant Unionists, led by Rev Ian Paisley, moderator of the Free Presbyterian Church. The party is essentially a reaction to the moderate policies of Capt O'Neill's premiership, but its candidates in the 1969 election were unsuccessful against official Unionists who (at a time of divisions within the Unionist Party) supported O'Neill. In the most dramatic intervention, Paisley stood against O'Neill in the Bannside constituency, and in a three-cornered battle the premier was elected on a minority vote. Paisley's position was strengthened by the disorders later in the year and by Protestant opposition to the far-reaching reforms forced upon Major Chichester-Clark. When O'Neill resigned after becoming a life peer in 1970, Paisley successfully contested the Bannside by-election on April 16, while a fellow Free Presbyterian clergyman was simultaneously successful in a by-election in South Antrim; neither, however, had an overall majority. Paisley's campaign was mainly concerned with law and order issues; he called for more effective policing of Catholic areas, and urged the rearming of the police and the recall of the Ulster Special Constabulary, an auxiliary force whose para-military security role had been taken over by the newly created Ulster Defence Regiment under the control of the British Army. It was to avoid this kind of splintering that Craigavon abolished proportional representation in 1929, and it is ironic that the Protestant Unionists might both have been defeated had there been a transferable vote system in 1970.

The 1969 election had also produced three independent or unofficial Unionist MPs who had stood successfully against candidates opposed or suspected of being opposed to O'Neill's policies and leadership. This liberal unionism received further impetus from the New Ulster Movement, a group of 'militant moderates' who backed some pro-O'Neill candidates in 1969, and from other ad hoc bodies set up in individual constituencies to back similar candidates. Soon after the Bannside and South Antrim by-elections, the Alliance Party of Northern Ireland was formed, drawing its initial support largely from these liberal unionist groups. It described itself as an alliance of Catholics and Protestants, an alliance of moderates committed to support of the constitutional link with Great Britain; it supported unequivocally the government's reform programme, but claimed to present 'a viable alternative to the existing splintered Unionist Party'. The Unionist Party was thus in danger of losing Protestant votes to both reactionary and reform parties, and even within the party there remained deep divisions; there was evidence of this on 24 April 1970, when the annual conference passed a resolution opposing a critical item in the reform programme, the proposal to set up a central authority in charge of all public housing.

One other point should be made about the Unionist Party. Its leaders accepted with reluctance the 1920 Act's provision for a separate parliament, for this appeared to represent some weakening of the ties with Great Britain. In a letter written in November 1921, Sir James Craig described it as a 'final settlement and supreme sacrifice in the interests of peace'. However, it was soon apparent to the Unionists that a local legislature provided an instrument which they could use to preserve and enhance the Protestant ascendancy in Northern Ireland. Following World War II, when Labour was in power at Westminster, some Unionists flirted with the idea of dominion status for Northern Ireland, but there has never been any significant support for suggestions that a better expression of unionism would be to give up Stormont and revert to the pre-1921 system of administration from Westminster. The annual report of the Unionist standing committee in 1936 made the point firmly :

> The cry 'Back to Westminster' is a subtle move fraught with great danger. Had we refused to accept a Parliament for Northern Ireland and remained at Westminster there can be little doubt that now we would be either inside the Free State or fighting desperately against incorporation. Northern Ireland without a Parliament of her own would be a standing temptation to certain British politicians to make another bid for a final settlement with Irish Republicans.

The guarantees in the Ireland Act, 1949, merely underlined for Unionists the importance which they attached to Stormont. The Nationalist Party and the Republicans each won six

seats in the 1921 general election, but refused to take their
seats in the new parliament. In 1925, the Nationalists won
ten seats and the Republicans two, and thereafter the Nationalists remained the largest opposition party. Their leader was
Joe Devlin, who had represented West Belfast at Westminster
for many years; he defeated Eamon de Valera there in 1918,
when the Irish parliamentary party held only six seats against
the upsurge of Sinn Fein. He also represented West Belfast
in the Northern Ireland Parliament, and took his seat there
after the 1925 election. Other Nationalists gradually followed
him, but the party was not prepared to become the official
opposition. However, the National League was formed in
1928, and Devlin became leader of the parliamentary party,
declaring : 'There is not, and there is not going to be, any
attempt of any kind, much less a conspiracy, to force the
people of Northern Ireland into a Dublin or any other
parliament'.

Inevitably, the Nationalists have found participation in
parliament a frustrating experience, for their primary political
objective—a united Ireland—proved unattainable. Devlin
himself was a skilled parliamentarian, and he and Craig had
great respect for one another, but the Unionists ultimately
adopted a more sectarian approach to hold the Protestant
vote together. Devlin described the abolition of proportional
representation as 'a mean, contemptible and callous attempt
by the majority which you now have to rob the minority . . .
of the safeguard which was incorporated in this measure'. In
fact, the Nationalists did not suffer electorally, as they had
done in local government several years earlier, but the effect
was to polarise politics. In *The Years of the Great Test,
1926-39*, David Kennedy wrote :

> . . . the simplest and surest way to rally Unionist voters
> was by identifying Catholicism with Nationalism and Natio-
> nalism with disloyalty. The slogan 'Not an Inch' proved
> to be the equilibrant of all the forces tending to disrupt the
> Unionist vote. But this slogan, and other anti-Catholic ones
> . . . inevitably widened the area of controversy.

The Nationalist Party found itself forced into the position of
spokesman for the Catholic minority in Northern Ireland,
and Devlin felt that in championing Catholic interests in the

prolonged controversy over the 1923 Education Act, he helped to make nationalism seem a sectarian force. 'I hate sectarianism as much as anybody,' he said. 'But anyone placed as I am, as the representative of my own people struggling to their feet and trying to hold their own, must be mixed up with all the tragedy of their position. But I never consented to be the leader of a Catholic party and I never will consent.'

However, Protestant nationalists were a comparatively rare phenomenon in Northern Ireland, and Catholics tended to see the whole Protestant community as willing partners in the religious discrimination practised by Unionist politicians. Moreover, advocates of a united Ireland often differed in tactics—the conservative and constitutional Nationalists contrasted with the more radical Republicans who accepted force as legitimate—and organisations like the National League, the Irish Union Association in the 1930s and the post-war Anti-Partition League were doomed to fail. On the whole, the Nationalists knew which Stormont seats they could win, and were content to contest these without making vain assaults on Unionist strongholds; they even yielded the Catholic areas of Belfast to representatives whose nationalism was blended with socialism. In *The Years of the Great Test, 1926-39*, J. L. McCracken concluded that the parliamentary representatives of the Catholic minority had put themselves in an impossible position :

> Whether they were, like Devlin, in the tradition of the old home rule party of John Redmond or whether they were out and out Republicans their basic aim was to secure a united Ireland. In other words they wanted to undermine the regime that had been established in the North by the act of 1920. That being so they could not play the role of an opposition in the traditional British manner; the relations between government and opposition which existed in Britain could not exist in the North even though the Northern parliament was modelled on the British one. . . .
>
> Certain consequences followed from this situation. It enabled—indeed it almost obliged—Unionists to appropriate loyalty and good citizenship to themselves and to use the national flag as a party emblem; it led, at least in the popular mind, to the identification of Catholicism with hostility to the state; it detracted from the effectiveness of opposition criticism of the government even on issues which had no bearing on

the constitutional question; and it encouraged irresponsibility, rashness and a narrow sectarian approach on the part of some Nationalist members. The Nationalists would undoubtedly have been more weighty as an opposition, they would probably have better served the interests of the minority and indeed of the whole community, they might have contributed to a better understanding between North and South if they had been prepared, even as a short-term policy, to accept fully and frankly the constitutional position as they found it—as De Valera did when he entered the Dail in 1927.

The 1960s brought some rethinking, prompted in part by the formation of a new movement called National Unity. Essentially this was an organisation of middle-class Catholics, and reflected the desire of businessmen and professional people to play a more constructive part in Northern Ireland life. It was oriented more to the Belfast area than the predominantly rural Nationalist Party, and while it ultimately failed to achieve a united front of parties in favour of a united Ireland, it did encourage the Nationalists to adopt a more disciplined approach to politics. In 1964, the Nationalists produced a substantial statement of party policy over a wide range of issues, and in February 1965—following Capt O'Neill's meeting with the Prime Minister of the Republic, Mr Lemass—assumed the role of official opposition at Stormont for the first time. In 1966, the party held the first of a series of annual conferences. The party's experience as 'Her Majesty's loyal opposition' was an unhappy one. Although the speaker of the House of Commons promised to accord 'the conventional courtesies due to the largest numerically Opposition party accepting the role', the government proved reluctant to embark on the sort of consultations that are commonplace at Westminster. In October 1968—following the outbreak of violence in Londonderry on 5 October, after the minister of home affairs had banned a civil rights march—the Nationalists gave up their role as official opposition. In the general election of 24 February 1969, the party lost three of its nine seats at Stormont to independent candidates prominent in the civil rights movement. The vote was perhaps a criticism of the party's concentration on the partition issue, when the civil rights cause presented more attainable objectives, but Nationalist spokesmen continued to argue that partition was the

root cause of evils in Northern Ireland society. As the 1970s
began, the party could still be characterised as 'green tories',
but some elements favoured more radical social policies.

Republicanism is a movement rather than a conventional
political party. Although the Republicans won six of the
twelve anti-Unionist seats in 1921, the Nationalist Party has
since borne the brunt of representing the Catholic minority
in the Northern Ireland Parliament. Republicans have been
reluctant to recognise Stormont even to the extent of contesting
seats on an abstentionist platform, and in recent years have
concentrated on Westminster seats. A factor in this was the
Representation of the People Act (NI), 1934, which required
candidates at nomination to declare an intention to take their
seats if elected. Under the Electoral Law Act (NI), 1962, candidates are required to declare that they 'recognise the lawful
authority of the Parliament of Northern Ireland'. However,
republicans are willing to condone and even encourage the
use of force to achieve their ideal of an Irish republic
embracing thirty-two counties, and the illegal Irish Republican
Army is as much a part of republican endeavour as any
electoral activity. The two elements can overlap, as in 1955,
when two Sinn Fein candidates successfully contested the
Westminster constituencies of Fermanagh-South Tyrone and
Mid-Ulster. Both men were serving prison sentences for their
part in an IRA arms raid on Omagh army barracks, and were
subsequently disqualified. (Under the 1962 Act passed at
Stormont, candidates in Stormont elections must make a
declaration that they are not for any reason disqualified from
taking their seats.)

Sinn Fein contested all twelve Ulster seats in the 1955
British general election, and this level of political activity
was paralleled by the campaign of violence launched by the
IRA in December 1956. However, none of the Republican
candidates—as they were subsequently called after Sinn Fein
had been declared an illegal organisation under the Special
Powers Acts—succeeded in topping the poll in any subsequent
election, and in the 1966 general election they stood in only
five seats. In the 1970 general election, the Republicans contested no seats. At that time, the republican movement was
deeply divided. On the one hand, a left-wing element favoured

F

radical policies, concentrating on areas of social discontent; on the other hand, some republicans favoured traditional military activity, and pointed to the failure to defend Catholic areas of Belfast during the disturbances in August 1969. Towards the end of that year, an IRA convention decided to end its ban on parliamentary activity; a breakaway group, refusing to recognise the parliaments in Dublin and Belfast then set up a 'provisional army council'. In January 1970, a Sinn Fein convention in Dublin voted to end the policy of abstaining from the parliaments in Ireland and Great Britain, but there was less than the necessary two-thirds majority. A motion pledging allegiance to the IRA then led to a walkout by those who were prepared only to give allegiance to the provisional army council.

Although the Nationalist Party and the Republicans are agreed in wanting an all-Ireland republic, they are divided on the means of attaining it and have come into conflict at some elections. On the whole, the Nationalists appear to have a surer command of Catholic votes, but the Republicans appear more unbending, and there have been occasions when Nationalist MPs decided not to defend their seats rather than risk a split Catholic vote after Republicans declared their intention to stand. This happened in the two-member constituency of Fermanagh-Tyrone in 1935, and in Fermanagh-South Tyrone and Mid-Ulster in 1955.

The Northern Ireland Labour Party has never done very well at the polls, and any gains it has made have usually proved vulnerable to sectarian politics. The labour movement has never been able to present a united political front, and the attitude of the party (and of individual party members) to partition has often provoked controversy. Other smaller parties have at different times included the word 'labour' in their names; the Republican Labour Party won two Belfast seats in the 1969 Stormont general election, as did the Labour Party. Labour's grip on the Protestant working class is tenuous at best, and liable to slacken whenever sectarian feelings are aroused or the constitutional issue seems particularly important. Under the Trades Disputes and Trade Unions Act (NI), 1927, trade unionists must 'contract in' if they wish to pay a political levy towards party funds; in Great Britain, trade unionists must take positive steps to 'contract out' if they are unwilling to contribute to the funds of the British Labour Party.

Labour won three seats in 1925, but with the abolition of proportional representation won only one seat in 1929. Britain's swing towards socialism in 1945 was barely reflected in Northern Ireland, but the party lost all its Stormont seats in the 1949 general election. The Irish Free State had taken its decision to become a republic, and the Labour Party decided that it could no longer equivocate on the constitutional issue. Consequently, a party conference declared its belief that 'the best interests of Northern Ireland lie in maintaining the constitutional links with the United Kingdom'. The party lost some support over this decision, and further suffered when the Unionists were able to make the election something of a plebiscite on partition. Recovery came slowly, and in 1958 Labour won four seats at Stormont. Its MPs were recognised as the official opposition by the speaker—though not by the government—and made a notable contribution to debates on economic and social issues. However, two of these seats were lost in the 1965 election, by which time the Nationalists had claimed the role of official opposition. In 1970, in an attempt to revitalise the party, a decision was taken to apply to become part of the British Labour Party. There has also been a greater readiness to discuss matters of common concern with other socialist parties in Ireland, including the Irish Labour Party in the Republic. However, contacts of this kind carry political risks for they can be represented as a weakening of Labour's position on the constitutional issue.

Labour's failure is that it does not command the broad spectrum of support enjoyed by its British counterpart. There is much less overt support from the professional and academic communities, and much of the Protestant working-class vote goes automatically to the Unionists or to more extreme candidates. During World War II, the Commonwealth Labour Party provided a more obviously 'loyal' alternative, and its leading figure, Mr Harry Midgley, ultimately joined the Unionists and became minister of education; today, there is a Unionist Labour movement. The influence of the Orange

Order, whose lodges fulfil the role of working men's clubs, is also significant. The existence of a Labour government at Westminster has never helped the fortunes of the Northern Ireland Labour Party; the Unionist administrations have been generously treated (a Labour government introduced the Ireland Act, 1949) and voters have had no reason to think that a Labour administration at Stormont would fare better.

None of the other political parties has carried much weight at elections. The Liberals held a university seat at Stormont for some years until the constituency was abolished, but have not been successful elsewhere. Their lack of support stems from the home rule crisis; Liberals today tend to adopt an equivocal attitude on the constitutional issue, accepting that a majority of people in Northern Ireland favour the union with Great Britain and preferring to discuss more pressing issues. The Communist Party has never been an important electoral force, though individual members are influential in the trade union movement. However, in August 1970, six MPs and one senator announced the formation of the Social Democratic and Labour Party; they included former members of the Labour, Republican Labour and Nationalist parties, as well as independents. The party described itself as anti-sectarian and promised policies based on 'radical left of centre principles'. It aimed to 'promote co-operation, friendship and understanding between North and South with a view to the eventual reunification of Ireland through the consent of the majority of people in the North and in the South'. An objective was to provide a strong opposition voice in case right-wing elements gained control of the government and interfered with the reform programme.

Outside party politics, a number of organisations can be said to exercise a political role or to influence the political environment. These include the Orange Order and its nationalist counterpart, the Ancient Order of Hibernians. They include illegal organisations like the IRA and its extreme Protestant counterpart, the Ulster Volunteer Force. They include a series of militant Protestant organisations and also groups which can be collectively described as the civil rights movement.

In *Orangeism: A New Historical Appreciation*, Rev S. E. Long wrote :

> The Orange contribution to politics has been seen by its beneficiaries as a great boon and by others as a largely hurtful influence which controls and contains Unionism to the distress of the minority. The influence of the Order on the Government is as real, and as proper, as the influence of any other responsible and loyal organisation. It is no discredit to the Institution that many Unionist politicians belong to it. It would be an indictment if these men were coerced by their membership. Many of the politicians were Orangemen long before they became M.P.s. That they act and think as Orangemen is understandable. There is no conflict of loyalty between that which the politician gives to the Government, Parliament and the Party and that which he gives to the Order.

The book is dedicated 'To the Glorious, Pious, and Immortal Memory of the Great and Good King William . . .' This is part of an orange toast, one version of which continues :

> . . . who saved us from Rogues and Roguery, Slaves and Slavery, Knaves and Knavery, Popes and Popery, from brass money and wooden shoes; and whoever denies this Toast may he be slammed, crammed and jammed in the muzzle of the great gun of Athlone, and the gun fired into the Pope's Belly, and the Pope into the Devil's Belly, and the Devil into Hell, and the door locked and the key in an Orangeman's pocket.

By contrast, the qualifications required of an orangeman before he is elected to a lodge demand that he

> . . . love, uphold, and defend the Protestant religion, and sincerely desire and endeavour to propagate its doctrines and precepts; he should strenuously oppose the fatal errors and doctrines of the Church of Rome, and scrupulously avoid countenancing (by his presence or otherwise) any act or ceremony of Popish worship; he should, by all lawful means, resist the ascendancy of that Church, its encroachments, and the extension of its power, ever abstaining from all uncharitable words, actions, or sentiments, towards his Roman Catholic brethren . . .

If orangeism exists to defend 'civil and religious liberty', this liberty is defined in terms of a Protestant ascendancy. Consequently the order must inhibit attempts to broaden the base of Unionist Party support and membership to include the Catholic community. The direct influence of the order appears much reduced in recent years, despite its substantial representation on the Ulster Unionist Council, but its indirect influence is substantial in that a large majority of Unionist MPs and senators belong to the order, as do many party members. However, aspiring Unionist politicians feel it less necessary than in the past to join the order, and when Dr Robert Simpson was named as Northern Ireland's first minister of community relations on 25 September 1969 he immediately announced his resignation from the order. He said he took this action to avoid any suggestion, however ill-founded, of improper influence. At this time, two other members of the cabinet were not orangemen; one had resigned when a member of his family married a Catholic, while the other had been expelled after attending a Catholic service held as part of a civic week in his constituency.

The Ancient Order of Hibernians fulfils within the Catholic community a social role not unlike that of the Orange Order. However, while the Orange Order brings together the different Protestant denominations, the AOH exists within a community already united by a single church exercising a broader social influence (for example, in education) than the Protestant churches do. Thus, the AOH is less influential, and on the political side cannot be said to be a major force in determining the course of Irish nationalism.

The Irish Republican Army first emerged as a guerilla force in 1919, and its small 'flying columns' harassed British forces very successfully. When the 1921 Anglo-Irish Treaty was ratified by the Dail on 7 January 1922, many IRA men accepted it; others took a different view, and civil war soon followed. It ended in 1923 with the defeat of the anti-treaty forces, and in 1926 there was a further split in republican ranks when Eamon de Valera resigned from Sinn Fein and founded the Fianna Fail ('Warriors of Destiny') party, whose members were prepared to take their seats in the Dail. A few months earlier, in November 1925, the IRA had withdrawn support from de Valera; it proceeded to set up an army council, responsible for directing the continued effort to end partition by force. In recent years, IRA activity has principally been directed at targets within Northern Ireland, particularly symbols of the 'British occupation'. A protracted campaign of violence began on 12 December 1956 and lasted until February 1962. The army council issued a manifesto at the beginning of the campaign :

> This is the age-old struggle of the Irish people versus British aggression. This is the same cause for which genera-tions of our people have suffered and died. In this grave hour, all Irish men and women, at home and abroad, must sink their differences, political or religious, and rally behind the banner of national liberation.

In fact, the campaign attracted little support north or south of the border, and both governments introduced powers of in-ternment. Other militant republican organisations were active at this time, and further divisions within republicanism have since developed. The movement is subject to recurring periods of heart-searching, simply because the policy of force has not succeeded; from time to time, elements choose to work instead within the institutions of government in both parts of Ireland. Patently, the IRA has not achieved its primary objective, and can be said to have failed as a political force in recent years. On the other hand, it has an important indirect influence on Ulster politics in that its activities keep the constitutional question to the forefront and help the Unionists to retain command of the Protestant vote.

It is only since 1966 that there has been a comparable organisation of extreme unionists or Protestants, the Ulster Volunteer Force. There was considerable Protestant unrest at this time, because the fiftieth anniversary of the Easter Rising in Dublin was being celebrated on a substantial scale. In May 1966, a UVF statement warned : 'From this day we declare war against the I.R.A. and its splinter groups. Known I.R.A. men will be executed mercilessly and without hesitation'. The following month, following the murder of two Catholics, the UVF was proscribed. Comparatively little is known about the organisation of the UVF, but it has continued to engage in terrorist activities on both sides of the border. In March and April 1969, there were explosions at a number of water and electricity installations in Northern Ireland, apparently designed to harden political attitudes and help to bring down the Prime Minister, Capt O'Neill; many people assumed that these were the work of the IRA or other republican extremists, and not until after O'Neill had resigned did it emerge clearly that the UVF had been responsible.

A number of other militant Protestant organisations have been active at different times during the past fifty years, but have remained within the law. The Ulster Protestant League was active in the 1930s. Towards the end of the 1950s, an organisation called Ulster Protestant Action summarised its purpose in these terms :

ULSTER—

Its field of activity is Ulster. Its great objectives are the *solving* of vital Protestant problems, the *strengthening* of Protestant bulwarks and the *stablishing* of new Protestant safeguards in order that our glorious Reformation Heritage may be preserved and our Province delivered from the slavery of a Roman Catholic Republic.

PROTESTANT—

Its basis and bond of union is Protestantism, the Protestantism of the Bible. It unflinchingly maintains the cardinal doctrines of Christianity as set forth in the Apostles' Creed and uncompromisingly denounces and resists all forms of Popery.

ACTION—

It is Ulster's Protestantism in Action. It operates by efficient organisation, effective propaganda and eternal vigilance. It resists by all lawful means every activity which would jeopardise our Protestant faith and heritage. Its purpose is to permeate all activities social and cultural with Protestant ideals and in the accomplishment of this end *it is primarily dedicated to immediate action in the sphere of employment.*

In recent years, an Ulster Loyalist Association has made a practice of celebrating the anniversary of the signing of the 1912 covenant. Civil rights demonstrations have incurred some resistance from another organisation, the Loyal Citizens of Ulster. The most influential body, however, is the Ulster Constitution Defence Committee.

The Ulster Constitution Defence Committee and the Ulster Protestant Volunteers which it governs is one united society of Protestant patriots pledged by all lawful methods to uphold and maintain the Constitution of Northern Ireland as an integral part of the United Kingdom as long as the United Kingdom maintains a Protestant Monarchy and the terms of the Revolution Settlement.

The committee, which was originally called together by Rev Ian Paisley, has twelve members. The Ulster Protestant Volunteers are organised according to Stormont parliamentary divisions, and only those who have been born Protestants are eligible for membership; each member must be prepared to pledge his first loyalty to the society even when its operations are at variance with any political party to which he belongs. The UCDC has provided an umbrella for much of Paisley's political activity, including his opposition to civil rights demonstrations. In 1969, the report of the Cameron Commission on *Disturbances in Northern Ireland* (Cmd 532) referred to a number of counter-demonstrations, and concluded:

> It is our considered opinion that these counter-demonstrations were organised under the auspices of the Ulster Constitution Defence Committee and the Ulster Protestant Volunteers and that their true purpose was either to cause the legal prohibition of the proposed Civil Rights or People's Democracy demonstrations by the threat of a counter-demonstration, or, if this move failed, to harass, hinder and if possible break up the demonstration.

The civil rights movement has taken various forms, but in each case there has been a predominance of Catholics. In 1963, the Campaign for Social Justice in Northern Ireland was founded in Dungannon, county Tyrone, to combat religious discrimination in the allocation of council housing; it has also devoted a good deal of attention to discrimination in employment. The Northern Ireland Civil Rights Association was founded in 1967, with a constitution modelled on that of the National Council for Civil Liberties in Great Britain. Its membership has, from the beginning, embraced people of very different political views; a number of local associations have been formed in different parts of Northern Ireland, following the disturbances in Londonderry on 5 October 1968. The same disturbances led to the formation of the People's Democracy; it was originally centred on Queen's University, Belfast, but it was not restricted to members of the university. It began as a broadly based student protest movement, without formal organisation, but developed into a more disciplined group of activists; its most prominent figures advocate an all-Ireland workers' republic. The Londonderry disturbances also led to

the formation of a broadly based Derry Citizens' Action Committee, which organised a number of substantial demonstrations in the city. In July 1969, the Derry Citizens' Defence
Association was formed after riots followed the annual orange
celebrations, and it took control of the city's Bogside area when
worse disturbances followed a month later. During the Belfast
disturbances of August 1969, citizens' defence committees
emerged spontaneously in Catholic districts, and vigilantes
maintained order in areas closed to police and troops. Some
Protestant areas also had defence associations, but these
seemed more an expression of militancy than of fears of attack.

The growth of the civil rights movement reflected a discontent with parliamentary and other democratic institutions. In
this, Northern Ireland was not unique; street demonstrations
had proved effective in other parts of the world, though they
might have different objectives. Leaders of the movement
professed non-violent methods, and many of them worked
hard to contain violence; the Cameron Commission even
noted that members of the IRA took part in demonstrations
and 'as stewards they were efficient and exercised a high degree
of discipline on marchers or demonstrators'. As the danger of
growing violence became apparent, there was a willingness to
turn to parliamentary action; four of the new MPs who won
seats in the 1969 Northern Ireland general election had been
prominent in civil rights demonstrations. However, the principal reforms designed to alleviate Catholic grievances came
only after violence; the disorders of August 1969 led to changes
much more profound than those which had contributed to the
resignation of Capt O'Neill earlier in the year. The effect of
the reforms was to meet—at least on paper—most of the
demands of moderates in the civil rights movement. This
tended to leave the initiative for further action with more
extreme elements, either the advocates of an all-Ireland
workers' republic or the more traditional republican elements;
the latter had tasted power behind the barricades of 'Free
Derry' and 'Free Belfast', and respect for authority (even when
reformed) patently declined.

4

Church and State

The existence of a plural society in Northern Ireland has posed problems throughout the past fifty years. Indeed, there are few major areas of administration in which the basic politico-religious division between Protestant and Catholic does not arise in some form. Arguably, some problems might more readily have been solved in a wider United Kingdom context, but they have instead been exacerbated by suspicion and distrust which exists between the two communities. Nor, until comparatively recently, has there been much real effort to improve community relations.

Law and order

The pattern was established early on, when Catholics stayed aloof from the institutions of a government they hoped and even believed could not survive—the boundary commission had still to report—while the Protestants determined to defend themselves against 'disloyal' elements by every possible means. With partition, northern Catholics who had formed part of a religious majority in Ireland became a minority inside the six counties; British rule was to a large extent replaced by local Protestant rule. The situation was made worse by the violence which reigned during the early 1920s, and which called for exceptional measures to restore law and order.

In 1836, a single police force was established in Ireland, and later became known as the Royal Irish Constabulary. Soon after the Northern Ireland Government was formed, a departmental committee recommended a similar northern

91

force with a strength not exceeding 3,000, one-third of the places being reserved for Catholics. The Royal Ulster Constabulary was set up by the Constabulary Act (NI), 1922, under the control of an inspector-general responsible to the minister of home affairs. However, Catholic recruitment never reached the proposed level, and in 1969 only eleven per cent of regular policemen were Catholics. There was, in addition, the Ulster Special Constabulary. Recruitment for the USC began on 1 November 1920, before the Northern Ireland Government came into existence, and initially there were three classes. Class A platoons were willing to serve full-time, and could be posted anywhere in Northern Ireland; class B platoons did part-time duty in their own localities; class C recruits were not readily available for training or duty, but could be called up in grave emergency. Both the RUC and the USC were armed, and the latter—overwhelmingly, if not entirely Protestant, and largely drawn from the Orange Order—achieved an early reputation for sectarian violence, being credited with killing a number of Catholics in 1921-2.

To this period belongs the Civil Authorities (Special Powers) Act (NI), 1922. The so-called Special Powers Act was originally intended to be a temporary measure, and it was at first renewed annually; in 1933, new legislation gave it indefinite duration. The Act was to an appreciable degree inspired by and modelled on the Restoration of Order in Ireland Act, 1920, which gave the British Government power to make stringent regulations. Section 1 of the Northern Ireland Act gives the minister of home affairs wide powers to 'take all such steps and issue all such orders as may be necessary for preserving the peace and maintaining order', and he may delegate these powers to his parliamentary secretary or to any officer of the RUC. All regulations not contained in the schedule to the Act as originally passed must be laid before both the Commons and the Senate; if either house presents an address to the governor within fourteen days, he may annul the regulation. Section 2 establishes a number of offences against the regulations and contains in sub-section 4 a comprehensive provision : 'If any person does any act of such a nature as to be calculated to be prejudicial to the preservation of the peace or maintenance of order in Northern Ireland and not specifically provided for in the regulations, he shall be deemed to be guilty of an offence against the regulations'. Section 3 provides that any alleged offence may be tried by a court of summary jurisdiction. Under section 6, anyone convicted under the Explosive Substances Act, 1883, of causing an explosion likely to endanger life or of attempting to cause an explosion with intent to endanger life may be sentenced to death. Until the repeal of section 5 in 1968, punishment by whipping could be imposed for a number of lesser offences concerned with explosives, firearms, arson and demanding with menaces.

Regulations under the Act empower members of the RUC to enter and search buildings without warrant, and to stop and search vehicles and persons. There is power to suppress the publication of literature 'prejudicial or likely to be prejudicial to the preservation of peace or the maintenance of order'. An officer of the RUC can authorise arrest without warrant and detention for not more than forty-eight hours for the purpose of interrogation. The minister can make an order restricting a person's movement, or providing for his internment; in such cases, there is provision for making representations to an advisory committee appointed by the minister. It should be noted, though, that the number of regulations in force at any one time has varied considerably according to the state of peace. Moreover, during the IRA campaign of 1956-62, an internee could secure his freedom by signing a declaration that, although he had been a member of an illegal organisation, he had now 'severed all connexion with it and I do not intend to have anything further to do with that organization or any other illegal organization, or assist them in any way in the future'. Alternately, he could declare that 'I have never been, am not now, and never intend to become a member of the I.R.A. or any other illegal organization, or to assist any such organization in the future, and I am prepared to go before a court, if necessary, and swear that this is the truth'. Some internees were released without making either declaration, and none were held by the time the IRA announced the end of its campaign.

In 1936, the National Council for Civil Liberties published the report of a commission of inquiry which concluded :

Firstly, that through the operation of the Special Powers Act contempt has been begotten for the representative institutions of government.

Secondly, that through the use of Special Powers individual liberty is no longer protected by law, but is at the arbitrary disposition of the Executive. . . .

Thirdly, that the Northern Irish Government has used Special Powers towards securing the domination of one particular political faction and, at the same time, towards curtailing the lawful activities of its opponents. . . .

Fourthly, that the Northern Irish Government, despite its assurances that Special Powers are intended for use only against law-breakers, has frequently employed them against innocent and law-abiding people, often in humble circumstances, whose injuries, inflicted without cause or justification, have gone unrecompensed and disregarded.

However, as F. H. Newark pointed out in *Ulster Under Home Rule*,

no one can doubt that the circumstances which the Act was framed to meet were truly alarming. . . . This period was not, of course, the first occasion on which Irishmen had resorted to the bomb and pistol to reinforce their political arguments, and the Special Powers Act should rightly be considered, not as a unique piece of legislation, but as taking its place in that long line of repressive statutes which the unsettled state of Ireland has called forth.

Even so, Harry Calvert took the view in *Constitutional Law in Northern Ireland* that

. . . the Act may be claimed to have gone further than was strictly necessary even at the height of the troubles. The justification for retaining it in the circumstances of today is lacking unless, as seems unlikely, it is anticipated that a challenge to the maintenance of public order greatly in excess of anything witnessed in recent years is imminent. Sporadic outbursts of political violence have continued to occur into the 1950's and 60's but they do not seem to have been of such proportions as to have posed problems of peace-keeping beyond the competence of the ordinary procedures of criminal law. In the most serious of them, the offenders have been prosecuted to conviction by ordinary process of law for breaches of the ordinary criminal law such as treason felony and murder. The Special Powers Act has been invoked to proscribe organisations suspected of criminal activities but it has not been claimed that their proportions were such as to have overtaxed the resources of the administration of justice in the normal course, or that prosecution to conviction on charges of criminal or seditious conspiracy was rendered impossible by intimidation of witnesses. Nor does it seem that the proportions of the evil to be combatted are such as to require running the risk of oppressing the innocent.

The Special Powers Act has proved an embarrassment to the British Government, which has had to enter a derogation from the obligations imposed by the European Convention of Human Rights. Consequently, the statement of reforms on 22 November 1968 included an announcement that the two governments had agreed that

(i) as soon as the Northern Ireland Government consider this can be done without undue hazard, such of the Special Powers as are in conflict with international obligations will as in the past be withdrawn from current use; but

(ii) in the event of the Northern Ireland Government considering it essential to re-activate such Powers, the United Kingdom Government will enter the necessary derogation.

During the disturbances of August 1969, a number of men believed to have republican sympathies were detained briefly under the Act for interrogation. In November 1969, an order was made banning a rugby match between Ulster and the South African Springboks, whose tour of the British Isles had been marked by anti-apartheid demonstrations. The Act was also used during 1969-70 to impose temporary restrictions on the sale of alcohol in Belfast.

Possibly the most controversial use of the Special Powers Act in recent years was an order made on 7 March 1967 proscribing 'republican clubs' or any like organisation howsoever described. The Minister of Home Affairs, Mr William Craig, said at the time that there were some forty clubs, a substantial proportion of whose members were connected with the IRA or Sinn Fein. He said the clubs had been formed to circumvent the ban on Sinn Fein, and were being used to recruit young people for active IRA work. The republican clubs continued to function quite openly, and it was not until June 1968 that three men were prosecuted at Magherafelt, county Londonderry, on charges concerned with membership of an illegal organisation and promoting its objects. Two magistrates dismissed the first summons on the grounds that the Crown had not proved that the club concerned was a threat to peace and order; they reasoned that a club could not be banned simply because of its name. In November 1968, the Court of Appeal rejected this view by a majority decision; but the Lord Chief Justice, Lord MacDermott, took the view that the 1967 order was far too vague and wide to come within even the extensive powers of section 1 of the Special Powers Act. The majority view was upheld in the House of Lords in June 1969—two of the five law lords dissenting— and the three men were subsequently convicted and given a conditional discharge.

As the Cameron Commission pointed out in its report on *Disturbances in Northern Ireland*, powers under the Act 'have on the whole been exercised with a view to suppressing the I.R.A. and obtaining information about its plans and activities. For this reason these powers, especially those to enter and search, have borne most heavily upon the Roman Catholic part of the population'. This is less true of other legislation designed to maintain public order, but there is no doubt that many Catholics feel that such legislation has not been invoked with impartiality. The most important measures are the Public Order Act (NI), 1951, and the Public Order (Amendment) Act, 1970. The 1951 Act was modelled on the British Public Order Act, 1936, though it omitted sections prohibiting quasi-military organisations and the wearing of uniforms signifying connection with a political organisation or objective. Section 1 of the Act required forty-eight hours notice of processions to be given to local police, except in the case of processions customarily held along a particular route. Under section 2, a police officer or head constable had power to restrict or re-route the procession if he believed there might be a breach of the peace or serious public disorder. In addition, the minister of home affairs could ban a procession or make a more general order prohibiting public processions or meetings in a particular area for up to three months. The British Act contained similar provisions, except that the 'chief officer of police' was required to take the necessary initiative, and in the case of a ban had to apply to the local council, which could make an order only with the consent of a secretary of state (in practice, the home secretary). In London, a commissioner of police applied directly to the secretary of state for permission to ban. Other parallels between the 1951 and 1936 Acts were in measures to deal with provocative conduct and the obstruction of public meetings. Only the 1936 Act contained provisions against the carrying of offensive weapons at a public meeting or on the occasion of a public procession. The 1951 Act gave a power to arrest without warrant upon 'reasonable suspicion' which was not contained in the British Act.

The 1970 amending Act had a tortuous course through parliament. It was debated for more than 100 hours, an exceptional experience at Stormont, and its passage was delayed first by an opposition walk-out and later by the priority given to reforms following the disorders of August 1969. The Bill, as first introduced during Capt O'Neill's premiership, was primarily designed to deal with the problem of counter-demonstrations; later, sections were added to deal with street sit-downs and the occupation of public buildings, both of which were tactics used by the civil rights movement. Section 1 of the Act makes it an offence, not merely as before to organise an unlawful procession, but to take part in one; the period of notice for processions is extended to seventy-two hours. Neither provision is exactly paralleled in British legislation, except that some local enactments require notice of processions and prescribe penalties for participation in banned processions. The government first proposed ninety-six hours notice, but compromised on this and accepted an opposition proposal to exclude trade union processions from the requirement to give notice; the minister is required, under separate legislation, to undertake certain consultations before exercising his power to ban processions.

Section 2 of the Act gives the minister new power to ban counter-demonstrations while allowing the original procession to continue. Section 3 makes it an offence to hinder, molest or obstruct a lawful procession, and police can require anyone suspected of being about to commit such an offence to reveal his name and address. The intention is to combat the sort of ambush which occurred during a civil rights march at Burntollet, county Londonderry, on 4 January 1969. There is no

G

exact parallel in British legislation. The same section also makes it a specific offence to sit down in a public place with the intention of obstructing traffic, and to trespass in a public building or refuse to leave after being asked by an 'authorised person'. These provisions were criticised by the government's opponents on the grounds that existing legislation was adequate. Sections 6 and 7 respectively parallel the 1936 Act's provisions governing political uniforms and quasi-military uniforms; the first was suggested by an opposition member, the second was designed primarily to deal with militant Protestants. Section 8 parallels a provision in the Prevention of Crime Act, 1953 and prohibits the carrying of offensive weapons in public; again the target was militant Protestants, who had carried cudgels at some demonstrations.

The Public Order (Amendment) Act (NI), 1970, can fairly be described as a turning point in Stormont legislation. Although some of its provisions were criticised by Catholics, it was apparent that the Act's main purpose was to strengthen the law in such a way that militant Protestants could be better contained. In addition, the Minister of Home Affairs, Mr Robert Porter, showed a willingness not apparent in his predecessors to respond constructively to opposition suggestions.

The problems which public order legislation seeks to solve are not simple ones in Northern Ireland. There is a long tradition of marching, and orange lodges were celebrating the Battle of the Boyne before the end of the eighteenth century; in 1832, legislation was passed in a vain attempt to prevent clashes between orangemen and Catholic 'ribbonmen'. In July 1935, there were serious riots in Belfast, and a dozen people were killed; in the preceding tension, the Minister of Home Affairs, Sir Dawson Bates, had first banned parades and then revoked the ban under pressure. Unionist ministers of home affairs have not always shirked banning Protestant processions from marching through predominantly Catholic areas where disorder might occur, but their political careers have sometimes suffered as a consequence. The number of marches and demonstrations has grown in recent years, first with the growth of militant Protestant opposition to the more moderate unionism of Capt O'Neill, then with the rise of the civil rights movement. In June 1966, Rev Ian Paisley led a parade to protest against 'romanising tendencies' in the Presbyterian general assembly; there were disturbances as he passed through a Catholic quarter of Belfast and outside the assembly itself. Since 1966, the republican Easter parades have been held in a tense atmosphere, and a number of bans have been imposed and sometimes flouted.

On 5 October 1968, a ban on a civil rights demonstration in Londonderry and police mishandling of the situation gave an impetus to the civil rights movement and began a chain of events which utterly changed Northern Ireland. Over the years, Catholics have felt that their right to demonstrate peacefully was less well protected than the Protestants' right. However, with the passing of the Public Order (Amendment) Act on 5 February 1970, the government lifted a ban on processions which had been imposed during the rioting of the previous August. It was apparent that, in future, there would be a greater reluctance to impose bans; instead, there would be an attempt to provide adequate police and military protection for peaceful demonstrations, while making any necessary use of the new legislative powers. However, there continued to be heavy demands on the police and military forces, and on 23 July 1970 processions were again banned until February 1971.

One other local measure is the Flags and Emblems (Display) Act (NI), 1954, which has no British counterpart. It provoked controversy at Stormont, but few prosecutions have arisen. Section 1 of the Act gives protection to the Union Jack, making it an offence to interfere by force with its display by an occupier on his own property. Section 2 empowers the police to require that an emblem (in practice, it is likely to be the tricolour of the Republic of Ireland) cease to be displayed if they apprehend that there may be a breach of the peace. The police are also empowered to enter land or premises, if necessary, to remove the emblem. Under the Act, the attorney-general must consent to any prosecution. The most eventful use of the Act was during the British general election in 1964, when police twice broke into the Republicans' election headquarters in West Belfast to remove a tricolour displayed in the window. Earlier, Rev Ian Paisley had threatened a protest march, but this was banned; the police raids in a predominantly Catholic area were followed by several nights of rioting.

There is also an Emergency Powers Act (NI), 1926, under which the governor may proclaim a state of emergency, whereafter the government can make whatever regulations it deems necessary. However, this Act is concerned with actions which, 'by interfering with the supply and distribution of food, water, fuel, or light or with the means of locomotion', may deprive the community of the essentials of life. In its evidence to the commission on the British constitution in 1969, the Ministry of Home Affairs noted :

> The seamen's strike of 1966 revealed a gap between the emergency powers of the Northern Ireland Government and those of Westminster in that Stormont's emergency powers are limited to use within Northern Ireland for the protection of the Northern Ireland community in respect of "transferred" services only and Westminster's emergency powers may be exercised only within Great Britain for the protection of the *Great Britain* community. The practical effect is that in an emergency affecting only Northern Ireland or in one affecting the whole of the United Kingdom, Stormont may not take action in respect of such "reserved" matters as merchant shipping, aerial navigation and the Post Office, whilst Westminster may exercise its powers only for the benefit of the community in *Great Britain*. Strictly speaking no ship or aircraft could be requisitioned, loaded with supplies and directed to carry them to Northern Ireland for the benefit of the community in Northern Ireland.

The civil disorders of 1968-9 led to a fundamental reorganisation of the police forces in Northern Ireland. The Cameron Commission made a number of specific criticisms of police behaviour, while recognising that 'In the majority of cases we find that the police acted with commendable discipline and restraint under very great strain and provocation from various quarters.' The commission referred to 'the feeling which undoubtedly exists among a certain proportion of the Catholic community, that the police are biased in their conduct against Catholic demonstrations and demonstrators', and added :

> Thus it is said that when the police have to interpose

themselves between Unionist demonstrators on the one hand
and a similar body of Catholic or Civil Rights demonstrators
on the other, they invariably face the latter and have their
backs to the former. The corollary is that if stones or other
missiles are thrown from the Unionist crowd the police do
not see who is responsible while they concentrate their attention against the non-Unionists. The fact is undoubted; the
reason given for it—that Unionists being loyalists do not
attack the police—is not accepted as satisfactory or a sufficient reply to the charge of partisan bias. This complaint
however is not confined to the events under investigation but
is one of general application and long standing.

There was widespread criticism of the police role in the
rioting of August 1969—which was subsequent to the period
covered by the Cameron Commission—and particularly of
the part played by the USC in Belfast and elsewhere. On 13
August, the Prime Minister, Major Chichester-Clark, announced that the USC would be used to the full, not for
riot or crowd control but to relieve the regular police of other
duties. However, this decision was revoked the following night,
when USC men were employed in riot situations for which
they had not been trained. Following talks between the
British and Northern Ireland governments on 19 August, a
small advisory committee was set up 'to examine the recruitment, organisation, structure and composition of the Royal
Ulster Constabulary and the Ulster Special Constabulary and
their respective functions and to recommend as necessary
what changes are required to provide for the efficient enforce-
ment of law and order in Northern Ireland'. The report of
the committee whose chairman was Lord Hunt, was published
in October (Cmd 535) and its major proposals were implemented. These included the following :

(1) The R.U.C. should be relieved of all duties of a
    military nature as soon as possible and its contribution
    to the security of Northern Ireland from subversion
    should be limited to the gathering of intelligence, the
    protection of important persons and the enforcement
    of the relevant laws.
(2) There should be a Police Authority for Northern
    Ireland, whose membership should reflect the propor-
    tions of different groups in the community.
(16) The present policy for the general issue and carrying
    of firearms should be phased out as soon as possible.

(18)   The effective strength of the force should be increased as a first priority.

(20)   A volunteer reserve police force should be set up.

(27)   Vigorous efforts should be made to increase the number of Roman Catholic entrants into the force.

(47)   A locally recruited part-time force, under the control of the G.O.C., Northern Ireland, should be raised as soon as possible for such duties as may be laid upon it. The force, together with the police volunteer reserve, should replace the Ulster Special Constabulary.

As the committee put it, 'Our proposals offer a new image of the Royal Ulster Constabulary as a civil police force, which will be in principle and in normal practice an unarmed force, having the advantage of closer relationships with other police forces in Great Britain'. Thus the military role of the RUC and the USC—commonly known as the B Specials, following the disbandment of the A and C classes—came to an end. A new part-time force, the Ulster Defence Regiment, was set up by Westminster legislation and became operational on 1 April 1970; it took over such traditional USC duties as guarding key installations and manning road blocks, and was wholly outside the control of the Northern Ireland Government. Initial recruitment suggested that about one-fifth of the regiment would be Catholics; a local committee was set up, with equal numbers of Protestants and Catholics, to advise on recruitment, and the applications of some USC members were rejected.

Education

Outside the field of law and order, the problems posed by Northern Ireland's plural society are no less complex. In particular, education has proved a source of recurring controversy, in which the Protestant and Catholic churches have played a prominent part. The Ministry of Education was established in June 1921, and three months later the minister, Lord Londonderry, appointed a committee under Mr Robert Lynn to 'enquire and report on the existing organization and administration of the educational services in Northern Ireland, and to make such recommendations as may be considered necessary for the proper co-ordination and effective carrying out of these services'. The committee, which was boycotted by Catholics, issued an interim report on 29 June 1922 and a final report on 19 June 1923. Three days later, the Education Act (NI), 1923, received royal assent.

The new ministry took over a three-stream schools system from Dublin on 1 February 1922. Hitherto, the Commissioners of National Education had controlled the national schools, which provided elementary or primary education; most of these schools were managed by clergy of different denominations, and the commissioners paid teachers' salaries and gave building grants for new schools. Secondary education was provided by intermediate schools, many of them profit-making concerns, which received grants from the Intermediate Education Board. Thirdly, there were technical schools, which were the responsibility of the Department of Agriculture and Technical Instruction, which also assisted the teaching of science and drawing in intermediate schools; the technical schools were controlled by committees of local authorities, and some costs were borne by the rates. In proposing the establishment of local education authorities, the Lynn committee assumed there was 'a general desire in the six counties that the local administration of education should be extended and strengthened', and pointed to the 'energy, generosity and administrative capacity which have been shown by local committees for technical instruction'. Certainly, many national schools could afford only minimal facilities, and the committee estimated that in expanding Belfast at least 12,000 children of school age were without places.

The 1923 Act made each county or county borough the responsible education authority for its area, acting through one or more education committees; initially, there were eighteen committees. Parents were required to ensure that children between six and fourteen years old received elementary education, which was defined as 'both literary and moral, based upon instruction in the reading and writing of the English language and in arithmetic'. Each committee had a duty to prepare schemes for the provision of elementary and secondary education; they were empowered to accept the transfer of existing schools from voluntary managers. However, the Act had ignored a recommendation of the Lynn committee that religious instruction should continue as before to be given in state-aided schools. Under section 28, such instruction was forbidden in elementary schools within the hours of compulsory attendance. Under section 26, local education authorities were not permitted to provide religious instruction in schools under their control, though they could provide opportunities outside school hours for children to be taught by persons approved by their parents. Under section 66, the education authority was not entitled to take into account a teacher's religious denomination when making an appointment. In *Episode in the History of Protestant Ulster, 1923-1947,* Very Rev William Corkey recalled Lord Londonderry telling representatives of the Protestant churches that

> all the quarrels between Roman Catholics and Protestants arose out of the teaching of the Bible and as he wished the children of all denominations to meet in the same schools and grow up in a friendly atmosphere he thought this could only be achieved if there was no Bible instruction and if Roman Catholic and Protestant children mixed in the same schools.

However, the Act also reflected an interpretation of the Government of Ireland Act, 1920, which was later abandoned. The evidence of the Ministry of Education to the commission on the British constitution makes the point :

> 3. The only provisions of the Government of Ireland Act which are directly relevant to the administration of the education system in Northern Ireland are those contained in Sections 5 and 8, which broadly provide (i) that the Government shall not endow any religion and (ii) that no person shall be afforded any advantage or suffer any disadvantage on account of religious belief.
> 4. In the 1920s difficulties arose from the interpretation of the prohibition against the endowment of any religion; the Ministry's legal advisers held that this meant that no public monies could be used to finance the giving of religious instruction in schools wholly financed from public funds, i.e. in schools provided by or transferred to the education authorities established under the Education Act of 1923. The Ministry's legal advisers, however, later revised the interpretation of what constituted "endowment of religion".

The major churches all opposed the Act. It is unlikely that any system of state education would have been acceptable to the Catholic Church, certainly not in the political climate of the period. The Protestant churches recognised this, and they were primarily concerned to ensure that Protestant teachers taught the Protestant children who would attend transferred or provided schools, and that Bible lessons would continue to have a place in the curriculum. Under pressure from the united education committee of the three main Protestant churches, and from the Orange Order, the government passed an amending Act in 1925 deleting the offending parts of sections 26 and 66. However, the Ministry of Education continued to take the view that education authorities could not provide and pay for religious instruction as defined in the 1923 Act, but advised that they could adopt a programme of 'simple Bible instruction' which teachers could be required to give as part of the ordinary school course. The 1925 Act paved the way for the gradual transfer of Protestant schools, but not all education committees were willing to accept the conditions of transfer which the Protestant churches sought to impose. The churches were also concerned about conditions in the growing number of provided schools, and the absence of any requirement to provide religious instruction.

The point was met in the Education Act (NI), 1930, section 4 providing that 'It shall be the duty of the Education Authority to provide Bible instruction, should the parents of not less than ten children who are in regular attendance at such school make application to the Education Authority for that purpose'. Section 4 obliged teachers to give Bible instruction, if so required by the education authority, but they could not be required 'as a condition of appointment or holding office, to teach any religious catechism or religious formulary which is distinctive of any particular religious denomination'. The Act also empowered the ministry to nominate as representatives of transferors up to one-quarter of the members of education committees. The transferors were also to be represented on the management committees of their former schools, where they could influence the short-listing of applicants for teaching posts. The Catholic Church remained unwilling to transfer any of its schools. However, the 1923 Act had provided for voluntary schools accepting 'four and two' management committees, with the education authority nominating one-third of the members; in return, certain expenses could be met from public funds. Proposals were put to the minister to make 'four and two' committees more acceptable to Catholics, but these were rejected. However, the government did provide for fifty per cent grants towards the building and equipping of voluntary schools, and the Catholic community was the major beneficiary. On the other hand, the Catholics were contributing through rates and taxes to the financing of an essentially Protestant system of state schools, and, as J. J. Campbell wrote in *Catholic Schools*, 'the 1930 Act was regarded by the Protestant churches as a "contract" by which the government satisfied the just demands made in conscience by the Protestant churches . . . the just demands made in conscience by the Catholic Church were not satisfied'.

Controversy broke out again towards the end of World War II, as the government prepared for a major reorganisation of education along similar lines to the Education Act, 1944, in Great Britain. In December 1944, a White Paper announced that the government was satisfied that

> it is proper that the right of individual conscience should be respected; it is also incumbent upon the Parliament of Northern Ireland to have strict regard to the prohibition contained in the Government of Ireland Act 1920, against passing a law which would, directly or indirectly, impose a disadvantage on account of religious belief. It is accordingly proposed that the liberty of conscience of an individual teacher in a school under the management of an education authority should be appropriately safeguarded in respect of the giving of religious instruction.

The following month, the Attorney-General, Mr William Lowry, questioned the legality of the deeds of transfer of Protestant schools, where the former managers had imposed conditions about religious instruction and the selection of teachers. The government carried its point in spite of bitter criticism, and the Education Act (NI), 1947, forbade committees taking into account ability to give religious instruction when making appointments in county schools. Nor were teachers to suffer any loss of promotion or other advantage through not giving religious instruction. However, the Act did make it compulsory for primary and secondary schools to provide undenominational religious instruction and a collective act of worship; consequently, there had to be provision for education committees to appoint an additional teacher to give religious instruction if none of the other appointees was suitable or willing.

As the Education Bill passed through Parliament, even stronger criticism was directed against a proposal to increase the aid to voluntary schools. In the 1944 White Paper, the government suggested increased grants to assist the post-war building programme, provided 'four and two' committees were accepted. These committees were unacceptable to all but a few voluntary managers, so the minister of education yielded and provided sixty-five per cent grants for new buildings and reconstruction, and for heating, lighting, cleaning and maintenance. Education authorities were also required to provide free such items as transport, milk and meals, and medical inspection. The minister, Col S. H. Hall-Thompson, was attacked from both sides of the House of Commons; Unionists accused him of endowing the Catholic Church, while Nationalists found the settlement ungenerous, though it was better than the fifty per cent grants available to church schools in Great Britain. While much of the controversy centred on primary schools under Catholic clerical management, a substantial number of Protestant voluntary grammar schools benefitted; it was obvious that they needed generous grants, if they were to retain their voluntary status and their long tradition of independence, and this helped to gain acceptance of the higher level of grants throughout the educational system. To claim capital grants, voluntary grammar schools had to undertake to reserve annually not less than eighty per cent of their admissions for 'qualified' pupils, those who had passed the new 'eleven-plus' examination. They became known as Group A schools; qualified pupils had their tuition fees paid by the education authority, but had to pay a capital fee towards the school's share of capital costs. Group B schools had no restrictions on admissions, though in practice most pupils would be qualified, and received capital grants only on accommodation for school meals. Some Protestant grammar schools were transferred to education authorities—now reduced to eight, corresponding to the counties and county boroughs—and new county grammar schools were built as needed.

The radical change in the 1947 Act, which came into operation on 1 April 1948, was the introduction of secondary intermediate schools for the academically less gifted who did not go to grammar schools; all-age elementary schools were gradually phased out, a process begun in England some years earlier. The building of new intermediate schools, or the conversion of existing primary schools, naturally put a heavy burden on the Catholic community; Protestants enjoyed free education at county schools. Although the government managed to put the Act on the statute book, there remained a reservoir of hostility towards Col Hall-Thompson, and he was sacrificed two years later when the new national insurance scheme required a decision on who should pay the employer's contribution towards insurance stamps for teachers in voluntary schools. The minister, initially with the government's support, took the view that because the state paid the salaries it should pay the employer's contribution. Under pressure from the Orange Order and Unionist backbenchers, the government yielded and the minister resigned. His successor, Mr Harry Midgley, resolved the problem by making the state responsible for sixty-five per cent of the employer's contribution; the remainder was to be paid by the voluntary managers or, where there was a 'four and two' committee, by the local authority. The government also promised a review of the whole system, but there has been no reversal of the trend towards increasing financial assistance for voluntary education, and in the next major educational controversy the government had really only to contend with Catholic critics.

It came over the Education (Amendment) Act (NI), 1968, which was preceded by a White Paper on *Local Education Authorities and Voluntary Schools* (Cmd 513), published on 19 October 1967. The latter proposed a new 'maintained' status for voluntary primary and intermediate schools which were prepared to accept 'four and two' committees; they would receive eighty per cent building grants, and the education authority would become responsible for all maintenance and equipment. Schools already under a 'four and two' committee (the committee could have more than six members) would have the option of reverting to purely voluntary management within a reasonable period, but thereafter the acceptance of maintained status would be irrevocable. Existing schools could remain under purely voluntary management, attracting sixty-five per cent grants, as could new schools which replaced them; but entirely new schools would be recognised for grant purposes only if they accepted 'maintained' status. In the case of Group A voluntary grammar schools, there was a similar proposal for eighty per cent building grants if the governing body accepted 'an appropriate measure of public representation', the minister of education nominating not more than one-third of its members after consulting both the governing body and the education authority. Entirely new voluntary grammar schools would only be recognised as grant-aided on these terms.

The Catholic Bishop of Down and Connor, Dr William Philbin, criticised the White Paper on the day it was published :

> It seems that an application by us to have State aid to Catholic schools brought up to the English level—65 per cent to 80 per cent—has been made the occasion of an invasion of the established system of Catholic school management. . . . We have to take account of the strongly-supported campaign against the existence of our schools in recent years, and to ask ourselves whether the present move is not seen as a first step towards their disappearance. No educational considerations appear to have been operative in this aspect of the proposed changes. The motives have been political and belong to the darker area of politics, in which religious prejudice is paramount.

The Catholic Primate of All Ireland, Cardinal William Conway, was more moderate in his comments when he returned from Rome on 1 November. He found some of the proposals in the White Paper very acceptable, but expressed concern at the power which it was proposed to give local authorities, whose new responsibilities would include equipment and external maintenance. 'If they treat us unfairly in such matters as housing—as many of them do—may they not do the same thing with our schools?' Negotiations with the Minister of Education, Capt William Long, proved abortive, and on 27 November Dr Conway and the northern bishops said the minister had turned down their proposal that he should nominate the public representatives on management committees and that these committees should retain the right to maintain and equip schools. When the minister commented that the statement indicated 'an almost complete rejection of the White Paper proposals', Dr Conway replied that 'A more accurate description would be almost total acceptance'.

The Bill was published on 6 January 1968, and included an important concession in that schools which accepted 'maintained' status would be free to revert to purely voluntary status. Former managers would have to give two years' notice of change, and during this period they would have to make appropriate repayments to offset the additional assistance they had received in respect of building, equipment and external maintenance. On 7 January, the Catholic bishops renewed their criticism, concentrating on two points, the far-reaching powers being given to local authorities—'much more extensive in several respects than the corresponding powers given to local authorities in Britain'—and the refusal to allow entirely new schools to opt out of 'maintained' status. In reply, the Ministry of Education pointed out that the Bill 'simply says that the Authority shall be responsible for the maintenance of the school premises and for defraying the expenses of carrying on the school, with some specified exceptions. How the Authority is to carry out its duty in detail is left to be determined by statutory regulations and by the terms of the formal schemes governing the setting up of the school committees'. The government stood firm on the Bill, which became law in March, but negotiations on a model scheme for 'the constitution, procedure and functions of a school committee for a maintained school' were successfully concluded in May. Under the scheme, which was accepted by the association of education committees, school committees have a responsibility to submit proposals on equipment and maintenance, and are responsible for safeguarding equipment; school committees are responsible for appointing teaching staff, while education committees are obliged to accept their recommendations on the appointment of ancillary staff, who act under the direction of the school principal. The bishops continued to have some reservations, but were prepared to give the new system 'a fair trial . . . in the interests of harmony and goodwill'. In the case of voluntary grammar schools, where there was general approval of the new Act, the move to eighty per cent grants proceeded rapidly.

How real is the Catholic fear of losing control of voluntary schools? On 8 April 1966, during a major speech on community relations at an ecumenical conference at Corrymeela, county Antrim, Capt O'Neill said :

> A major cause of division arises, some would say, from the de facto segregation of education along religious lines. This is a most delicate matter and one must respect the firm convictions from which it springs. Many people have questioned, however, whether the maintenance of two distinct educational systems side by side is not wasteful of human and financial resources, and a major barrier to the promotion of communal understanding.

On 20 April, Cardinal Conway noted that the prime minister had spoken on the subject of denominational schools four times within two years 'suggesting with varying degrees of emphasis that it would be a good thing for the community if Catholic schools were to disappear. . . . I find this continuing pressure on Catholic schools by the head of the Government very surprising and, indeed, disquieting'. There has not been any firm indication in recent years that the government would be prepared to take positive steps to end the division between Catholic and Protestant or state schools; quite apart from Catholic opposition, which it would hardly ignore, any change would raise the old controversy about Protestant children being taught by Protestant teachers. However, there is no doubt that the Catholic laity find voluntary education a burden; during the 1968 controversy, the Catholic bishops said that 'A conservative estimate would indicate that since the passing of the 1947 Education Act the Catholic community has contributed something in the region of £20 million in present-day money values towards the erection and maintenance of their schools'. In 1967, a survey carried out by National Opinion Polls Limited for the *Belfast Telegraph* indicated that about two-thirds of the electorate thought that Catholics and Protestants should be educated in the same schools; the figures showed little variation between the major religious denominations. In April 1970, the annual conference of the Unionist Party passed a resolution—against the advice of the Minister of Education, Capt Long—urging the immediate integration of all schools in the interests of future understanding and the necessity to live together. The minister described the resolution as impracticable.

The Mater Hospital

The Mater Infirmorum Hospital in Belfast provides another example of recurring controversy over state aid to a Catholic institution. The hospital was founded in 1883 to provide 'relief for the sick and suffering without distinction of creed', and there has always been an appreciable proportion of non-Catholics among its patients, particularly in the extern department. At the same time, Catholic medical principles prevail, and there is provision for ministering to spiritual as well as physical needs. After World War II, the Northern Ireland Government prepared to introduce a state health service on the British model, and the Health Services Act (NI), 1948 broadly corresponds to the National Health Service Act, 1946. Section 61 of the British Act provided that

> where the character and associations of any voluntary hospital transferred to the Minister by virtue of this Act are such as to link it with a particular religious denomination, regard shall be had in the general administration of the hospital and in the making of appointments to the Hospital Management Committee to the preservation of the character and associations of the hospital.

The Northern Ireland measure, which set up a Hospitals Authority, also contained provisions for maintaining the character and traditions of transferred hospitals. However, the Minister of Health, Mr William Grant, was unwilling to follow the British Act in providing for voluntary hospitals which wished to remain outside the state scheme to receive grants. Although it was pointed out that the Catholic authorities could not alienate the property, the minister offered only a simple option : 'They are either coming in 100 per cent, or they are staying out 100 per cent. There is going to be no half-way stage about this matter'. The Mater (as it is commonly known) opted out, and was 'deemed not to be a hospital for the purposes of any of the provisions of this Act'. Denied public funds, it actually lost some assistance it had hitherto received in respect of such items as nurses' salaries and the treatment of venereal disease.

For Catholics, it was an issue of conscience comparable to the education issue. Their case for assistance rested on the fact that the Mater, the only acute hospital in north Belfast, provided beds and services which reduced the burden on the Hospitals Authority. It was also a teaching hospital, unlike any of the 'disclaimed' hospitals in Great Britain which were state-aided; the importance of teaching hospitals had been recognised in the British Act, which provided for direct government finance outside the control of regional hospital boards. The Mater's status as a teaching hospital associated with the Queen's University of Belfast was negotiated as part of a settlement under the Irish Universities Act, 1908, and it was looked on as part of the educational inheritance of Ulster Catholics. To the Catholic community as a whole, though, the maintenance of a single voluntary hospital must seem less important than the maintenance of a whole system of separate schools; there is no canon law requiring attendance at Catholic hospitals. While the Catholic pupil always benefitted from public funds, the patient entering the Mater forfeited all claim to the free treatment and free medicines so readily available at other hospitals or from his general practitioner. Only a resourceful fund-raising operation ensured the hospital's survival—the major contribution has come from football pools, from which the government has levied duty— and in some cases salaries have been lower than in state hospitals.

In 1955, a committee under the chairmanship of Dr H. G. Tanner published its report (Cmd 334) on the health services in Northern Ireland. The committee argued that the Mater, so long as it remained outside the state service, had no right or entitlement to state aid, but added :

> Nevertheless, it is incongruous that the Mater Hospital should be prevented from entering into mutually beneficial relations with the State service by being declared 'not to be

H

a hospital' for the purposes of the Acts, and we recommend that this technical bar should be removed. There are numerous occasions when contact between the Hospital and the State service is bound to be desirable. To mention only one, there is the question of civil defence arrangements, which clearly call for co-operation on the part of all hospitals.

The Tanner committee rejected the idea of an annual state subvention to the hospital, on the grounds that it was not providing services for or on behalf of the Hospitals Authority. Instead, it recommended a limited form of contractual relationship under which the authority would have prior claim to a proportion of beds; admissions to these beds would be made from the authority's waiting lists, and the authority would pay the full cost of treatment and accommodation. The report added :

> The present isolation of the Mater Hospital seems to us a misfortune for the hospital itself and in lesser degree for the State service. It is not merely a matter of finance; the Hospital has found at least a partial, and perhaps in the long run a complete, answer to that aspect of its difficulties. There are other and subtler losses, not least of which is the absence of that easy, informal intercourse between individuals and groups and organisations which in general animates the State services in Northern Ireland and elsewhere in the Kingdom. We believe that a contractual relationship such as we have described would help to renew contacts and re-establish a sense of fellowship in a common cause.

The report referred to 'a strong feeling among the medical staff that they were being penalised by the State or its servants for the stand taken by the Board of Management'. In only one instance had an application for a post advertised by the Hospitals Authority been successful, and the applicant already held a post in one of the hospitals concerned. There was no doubt that the medical staff had suffered financially from the Mater's decision to opt out—as well as lower salaries, they had reduced opportunities for private practice—but the committee found 'no evidence to substantiate allegations of unfair discrimination'. (According to the Campaign for Social Justice, only 31 out of 387 specialist doctors employed by the Hospitals Authority in 1967 were Catholics.)

The question of aid remained dormant until Capt O'Neill

became prime minister, and it seemed that the government might make a gesture of reconciliation. However, there was opposition among Unionist backbenchers, and the Minister of Health and Local Government, Mr William Morgan, told the Commons on 18 February 1964 that he could see no real solution short of the hospital entering into the state scheme. However, the Tanner committee had recommended a change in the status of the Hospitals Authority, to make it an agent of the ministry—as were regional hospital boards in Great Britain—rather than a semi-autonomous body with considerable policy-making powers. The minister began to prepare legislation to implement this recommendation and to remove the technical bar to a contractual relationship with the Mater, and told the Commons on 9 March 1965 that he hoped it would be in effect by April 1966. Mr Morgan said it would be unreasonable to expect the Mater authorities to enter into any firm commitment until the new legislation had taken shape and was well on its way to coming into effect.

On 29 April, the Catholic Bishop of Down and Connor, Dr Philbin, published the text of a letter to Mr Morgan in which he accused the Ministry of Health and Social Services of a 'complete volte-face', suggesting that the ministry had reversed its previous willingness to preserve the identity of the Mater as a Catholic hospital in the state service. The minister was accused of publishing without consultation an account of negotiations which had hitherto been treated as strictly confidential; it was revealed that these negotiations, begun after the statement of 18 February 1964, had come to a halt in May and that there had been no government reply to requests for their resumption. Dr Philbin commented : 'I find this situation an extraordinary breach of accepted human relations, not to speak of official propriety'. In his reply, Mr Morgan said the bishop's letter contained inferences and implications concerning the attitude of the government which were inaccurate and misleading; the government felt that 'the issue of a letter in terms which call the Government's intentions and good faith into serious question does nothing to ease the situation or to promote any final and equitable settlement'. On 5 May, he told the

Commons that no solution of the problem was immediately in sight, and warned : 'With the increasing complexity of modern scientific medicine, the disadvantages of clinical isolation will grow, perhaps to the point at which, in the long run, the hospital's position as a teaching institution could be jeopardised.' However, negotiations were not resumed, and it was not until 17 January 1967 that a Bill was published, removing the bar on contractual relations with an 'exempted' hospital and providing a guarantee on similar lines to the British Act about preserving the character and associations of a denominational hospital. The passing of the Health Services (Amendment) Act (NI), 1967, led to the resumption of negotiations, but these were protracted and three years later a settlement had not been reached.

Religious discrimination

Allegations of religious discrimination against Catholics have been commonplace during Northern Ireland's years of self-government. These have been directed more often at local authorities than at the government, but even then it was an implicit criticism of the government for not taking remedial action. In a sense, the Unionists were merely dispensing political patronage to Protestant supporters in a manner that would be understood in many parts of the world; they had a further incentive in that they looked on Catholics as 'disloyal' citizens who were prepared to undermine the institutions of government and to alter the constitutional position if they ever achieved a majority position. Some Catholics, at least, were unwilling to participate in the processes of government —particularly since they would inevitably find themselves in a minority role, and perhaps be described as 'Castle Catholics' (an allusion to the former administration in Dublin Castle). Whatever the factors, the broad pattern of the divided society was clear. To take one example, a survey published by the Campaign for Social Justice in 1969 gave figures on the membership of public boards; many of the members were directly nominated by the government, but in some cases they represented specific interests.

	Total Membership	Catholics
Electricity Board for NI	5	0
Housing Trust	7	1
Craigavon Development Commission	9	1
Economic Council	18	2
Hospitals Authority	22	5
General Health Services Board	24	2
Medical Advisory Committee to the Ministry of Health	11	1
Pigs Marketing Board	14	2
Milk Marketing Board	13	1
Seed Potato Marketing Board	14	1
Agricultural Wages Board	15	2
Youth Employment Service Board	18	3
Fire Authority	16	0
Child Welfare Council	22	6
Ulster Folk Museum Trustees	20	1
Tourist Board	11	3
Advisory Council for Education	16	5
Council for Education Research	27	5
Youth and Sports Council	20	6
Industrial Court	22	1
Lowry Commission to redistribute Four University Parliamentary Seats	5	0
1969 Commission to Overhaul Stormont Parliamentary Boundaries	3	1

In public employment, the survey cited figures to show a similar predominance of Protestants in senior positions; they covered such fields as the health services, the police, the administration of justice, schools inspectors and the administrative, professional and technical grades of the civil service.

The Cameron Commission, in citing the general causes of the disturbances it investigated, put particular emphasis on local government :

(1) A rising sense of continuing injustice and grievance among large sections of the Catholic population in Northern Ireland, in particular in Londonderry and Dungannon, in respect of (i) inadequacy of housing provision by certain local authorities (ii) unfair methods of allocation of houses built and let by such authorities, in particular, refusals and omissions to adopt a 'points' system in determining priorities and making allocations (iii) misuse in certain cases of discretionary powers of allocation of houses in order to perpetuate Unionist control of the local authority . . .

(2) Complaints, now well documented in fact, of discrimination in the making of local government appointments, at all levels but especially in senior posts, to the prejudice of non-Unionists and especially Catholic members of the community, in some Unionist controlled authorities . . .

(3) Complaints, again well documented, in some cases of deliberate manipulation of local government electoral boundaries and in others a refusal to apply for their necessary extension, in order to achieve and maintain Unionist control of local authorities and so to deny to Catholics influence in local government proportionate to their numbers . . .

(4) A growing and powerful sense of resentment and frustration among the Catholic population at failure to achieve either acceptance on the part of the Government of any need to investigate these complaints or to provide and enforce a remedy for them . . .

The commission gave figures to indicate the effect of manipulating boundaries in areas where there had been disturbances :

Local authority	Population Census 1961		Council representation as at 30 September 1968	
	Adult Catholics	Adult others	Non-Unionists	Unionists
Armagh UDC	3,139	2,798	8	12
Dungannon UDC	1,845	2,041	7	14
Dungannon RDC	7,329	7,476	6	13 (plus 3 co-opted members)
Fermanagh County Council	15,884	15,222	17	33 (plus 2 co-opted members)
Londonderry County Borough	18,432	11,340	8	12
Newry UDC	5,843	1,364	12	6
Omagh UDC	2,605	1,949	9	12

The commission commented :

The most glaring case was Londonderry County Borough where sixty per cent of the adult population was Catholic but where sixty per cent of the seats on the Corporation were held by Unionists. These results were achieved by the use, for example, of ward areas in which Unionist representatives were returned by small majorities, whereas non-Unionist representatives were returned by very large majorities. In

Londonderry County Borough there was the following extra-ordinary situation in 1967:

	Catholic Voters	Other Voters	Seats
North Ward	2,530	3,946	8 Unionists
Waterside Ward	1,852	3,697	4 Unionists
South Ward	10,047	1,138	8 Non-Unionists
	14,429	8,781	20

23,210

The commission was satisfied that the six Unionist-controlled councils used their power to make appointments in a way that benefitted Protestants :

In the figures available for October 1968 only thirty per cent of Londonderry Corporation's administrative, clerical and technical employees were Catholics. Out of the ten best-paid posts only one was held by a Catholic. In Dungannon Urban District none of the Council's administrative, clerical and technical employees was a Catholic. In County Fermanagh no senior council posts (and relatively few others) were held by Catholics: this was rationalised by reference to 'proven loyalty' as a necessary test for local authority appointments. In that County, among the seventy-five drivers of school buses, at most seven were Catholics. This would appear to be a very clear case of sectarian and political discrimination. Armagh Urban District employed very few Catholics in its salaried posts, but did not appear to discriminate at lower levels. Omagh Urban District showed no clear-cut pattern of discrimination, though we have seen what would appear to be undoubted evidence of employment discrimination by Tyrone County Council.

It is fair to note that Newry Urban District, which is controlled by non-Unionists, employed very few Protestants. But two wrongs do not make a right; Protestants who are in the minority in the Newry area, by contrast to the other areas we have specified, do not have a serious unemployment problem, and in Newry there are relatively few Protestants, whereas in the other towns Catholics make up a substantial part of the population. It is also right to note that in recent years both Londonderry and Newry have introduced a competitive examination system in local authority appointments.

In the cash social services, the Northern Ireland Government has followed a 'step by step' policy, but there was one abortive attempt to depart from Westminster practice. In 1956, the British government increased family allowances; the rate had been 40p (96c) for the second and subsequent children in a family, but for the third and subsequent children became 50p ($1.20). The Northern Ireland Minister of Labour and National Insurance, Mr Ivan Neill, proposed to distribute the money at his disposal in a different way : 48p ($1.14) for the second and third children, and 40p as before for the fourth and subsequent children. Smaller families would benefit more than in Great Britain; larger (presumably Catholic) families would benefit less. Mr Neill took the view that family allowances were not required 'with a view to bringing about any increase in our population. . . . In these circumstances the proper aim of a family allowance scheme in Northern Ireland should be to increase the standard of living for as many of our families as possible'. However, the proposal was widely criticised, even in Protestant circles, and Unionist MPs at Westminster advised the Prime Minister, Lord Brookeborough, that British opinion would be hostile. The government quickly gave way.

While Protestants and Catholics live partly separate lives in Northern Ireland, the state to some extent imposes a Protestant ethos on the Catholic minority. In such matters as Sunday observance and liquor licensing laws, it is the more puritanical Protestant outlook which prevails; the Protestant churches are influential in this respect, but there is a wider Protestant feeling that a stand must be taken against Catholic values. At different levels of society, this instinctive attitude has always proved an obstacle to dealing justly and dispassionately with Catholic grievances.

5

Economic and Social Policy

In 1965, the government published a report by its economic
consultant, Professor Thomas Wilson, on *Economic Development in Northern Ireland* (Cmd 479), together with a
statement indicating general acceptance of the report and an
intention to base upon it plans for economic development up
to 1970. Professor Wilson opened his report with these words :

> For some years Northern Ireland has combined a record
> of rising output with one of persistently heavy unemployment.
> The percentage out of work has usually been about four
> times the national average and since the war has been
> higher than in any region in Great Britain. This fact is well
> known. What may be less well known is that industrial
> production went up by 50 per cent between 1950-62, an
> annual rate of growth of about 3¾ per cent as compared with
> 2¼ per cent in the United Kingdom as a whole. As might
> be expected, gross domestic product, which also includes
> agriculture and the service industries, has risen more slowly
> in both countries than industrial production, but Northern
> Ireland is once more ahead with an average increase of 2.7
> per cent as compared with 2.1 per cent for the United
> Kingdom. Although real income a head is still about 25 per
> cent below the national average, it rose by about a third
> between 1951-2 and 1961-2. While precise accuracy is not
> to be expected in a statistical comparison of this kind, it would
> be hard to dismiss the broad conclusion that the rate of
> growth of production in Northern Ireland has been above
> the national average. Many signs of this large advance would
> be immediately apparent to anyone returning to the Province
> after an absence of some years.

Unemployment has been a pressing problem since the
1920s, when the annual average of unemployment varied
between 13.2 and 23.9 per cent of insured workers. In the

1930s, the annual average fluctuated between 20.6 and 28.3 per cent. The lowest recorded levels occurred during World War II, but since then unemployment has not often averaged less than six per cent. The Northern Ireland economy is an integral part of the British economy, and its fluctuations reflect fluctuations in Great Britain. The major decisions affecting the local economy are taken in Great Britain, and do not always provide for local needs; measures to counteract overfull employment and inflation in Great Britain have frequently retarded expansion in Northern Ireland. Patently, Northern Ireland suffers from its peripheral position within the United Kingdom, a position aggravated by the Irish Sea barrier. Its domestic market is small, and the partition of Ireland meant in some cases the loss of southern markets. Manufacturing industry has lacked substantial local resources of raw materials or fuel. Such industries as linen and ship-building, which were the basis of nineteenth-century growth, have tended to contract. Agriculture provides a diminishing number of jobs. Northern Ireland has suffered from having a smaller proportion of fast-growing industries than Great Britain, and its 'activity rate'—the proportion of the population in employment—is also appreciably lower. The population has also been increasing, though the excess of births over deaths has been substantially offset by outward migration; labour scarcity in the English Midlands and South East has encouraged this migration, just as it has helped the drive for new industry in Northern Ireland.

Intercensal period	Population at beginning of period	Excess of births over deaths	Intercensal increase in population	Net movement outwards
1926-37	1,256,561	80,835	23,184	57,651
1937-51	1,279,745	158,443	91,176	*67,267
1951-61	1,370,921	146,349	54,121	92,228
1961-6	1,425,042	97,434	59,733	37,701

(Figures from *Ulster Year Book 1969*.* includes deaths in the British services and merchant navy outside Northern Ireland.)

Aid to industry

With few economic powers at its disposal, the Northern Ireland Government has concentrated on providing direct aids to industrial development, and on occasions providing special assistance to existing industries in difficulties. In the latter category were the Loans Guarantee Acts (NI), 1922-38 and 1946, which empowered the minister of finance to guarantee the repayment of loans raised for the building of ships and other capital equipment; these Acts were particularly important during the 1930s in ensuring the survival of the Harland & Wolff shipyard in Belfast. More important, however, were the New Industries (Development) Acts (NI), 1932 and 1937. These Acts belonged to a period in which the British Government was also recognising a responsibility for encouraging employment in 'depressed areas'. The Northern Ireland Government also recognised a need for industrial diversification, and the local economy has in recent years become much less vulnerable to the effects of recession in a small number of industries. The 1932 Act empowered the government to offer certain new industries, producing goods not then being manufactured in Northern Ireland, grants equivalent to a reasonable annual rent on the sites they occupied. In addition, local authorities could grant exemption from rates. The 1937 Act also offered interest-free loans for the erection, purchase, renovation or adaptation of buildings for new industries, as well as interest-bearing loans for other purposes, including the expansion of existing industries. Patently, the two Acts were passed during a period when British industry as a whole was working below capacity; however, more than fifty firms took advantage of the assistance offered, and at the end of 1961 these pre-war establishments or expansions employed almost 5,500 workers.

New impetus was provided by the Industries Development Acts (NI), 1945-53, which empowered the Ministry of Commerce to provide on lease modern factory premises, to provide financial assistance to new industries or for the expansion of existing ones, and to aid the appropriate authorities in improving such basic services as roads, water supply, sewerage and power. Local authorities could grant rates exemption to assisted projects for a maximum of ten years. The ministry was given wide discretion in determining the nature and level of aid required to attract new industries; the normal grant towards capital costs was $33\frac{1}{3}$ per cent, although this could be exceeded for particularly attractive projects or reduced if the employment provided seemed low in proportion to the capital cost. Ministry factories were provided at a lower than economic rental, and a programme of advance factories meant that an interested firm could often be offered early occupation of premises in areas where a pool of labour existed.

To qualify for assistance, an applicant had to undertake a specific development with an agreed target of employment. The ministry had to be satisfied that ultimately the applicant could carry on without assistance. It also took into account such factors as the proportion of male workers to be employed, the location of the project in relation to unemployment levels throughout Northern Ireland, and its contribution to the diversification of industry. By the end of 1955, some 22,600 jobs had been provided by new firms and expansion schemes assisted under the 1945-53 Acts, and a further 9,800 jobs were anticipated in these assisted firms. The Industrial Development Act (NI), 1966, further extended the ministry's powers to assist new projects, and the basic grant towards the cost of new plant, machinery and buildings became forty-five per cent; this was actually increased to fifty per cent as a short-term measure until the end of 1968, and again for a three-year period following the disorders of 1969. Where a project offered exceptionally attractive levels of employment or was in an area urgently in need of industry, there was provision for grants towards operating costs in the initial period and for loan assistance. As before, firms were expected to provide an agreed amount of employment within a specified period.

As the 1945 Act began to take effect, the government found itself accused of neglecting traditional industries while assisting newcomers who in many cases offered much better wages and working conditions. Leaders of the linen industry had always been influential in the Unionist Party and indeed in the government, and the industry benefitted substantially from the Re-equipment of Industry Acts (NI), 1951 and 1953; these provided one-third grants for approved schemes of re-equipment and modernisation designed to increase firms' competitive efficiency. When the scheme closed at the end of 1953, 279 projects had been approved, involving grants of £3.5 million ($8.4 million). By contrast with the Industrial

Development Acts, there was no requirement to increase employment, and in fact modern machinery could lead to reduced employment.

There followed the Capital Grants to Industry Acts (NI), 1954-62, under which the ministry paid annual grants to industrial undertakings equivalent to a percentage of their annual net expenditure on certain new building work and on new plant and machinery. The rate of grant was raised from 25 to 33⅓ per cent in 1959, and normally was available for any items which qualified for investment allowance against income tax. No employment targets were required, and no specific schemes had to be undertaken. In the first ten years of the scheme, over £31 million ($74.4 million) was paid in grants. It was succeeded by the Industrial Investment (General Assistance) Act (NI), 1966, which provided for grants of forty per cent of expenditure on new plant, machinery and buildings. As with the Industrial Development Act (NI), this was increased by five per cent for a period until the end of 1968 and again after the 1969 disorders. The revision of the capital grants scheme was dictated by the passing of the Industrial Development Act, 1966, at Westminster. The British Act provided twenty per cent grants towards new plant and machinery, with forty per cent grants available in development areas, where unemployment was higher. The new grants replaced investment allowances; hitherto, industries in Northern Ireland had been able to take advantage of both grants and allowances, though the allowances could not be claimed on that proportion of the investment which was covered by grant. Since Northern Ireland's drive for new industries depended to some extent on being able to offer bigger incentives than the development areas, the Stormont Act included new buildings (not aided in Great Britain) and also provision for loans to assist firms with the re-equipment and re-housing of their operations. However, because the Ministry of Commerce adopted the same criteria for eligibility as the Board of Trade in Great Britain, some industries which had benefitted under the capital grants scheme ceased to receive aid.

The burden of transport costs across the Irish Sea was recognised by the Aid to Industry Act (NI), 1953, which provided an annual sum of £750,000 ($1.8 million) towards the costs incurred by manufacturing firms in acquiring coal or its equivalent in gas or electricity. Subsequent legislation extended the scheme to cover oil, and the sum available for distribution annually was raised to £1.1 million ($2.6 million). The Industrial Advice and Enterprise Acts (NI), 1964 and 1967, provided grants to manufacturing firms towards the cost of employing consultants to advise on ways to increase efficiency. The same legislation provided for a small Industrial Enterprise Fund, largely used to encourage management training; a non-profitmaking organisation, Management Development Services (Northern Ireland) Limited, has also been set up.

In matters falling within the competence of the British Government, Northern Ireland has been treated as a development area. Thus the Board of Trade, in issuing industrial development certificates for new manufacturing premises, would bear in mind Northern Ireland's employment needs. Similar tax concessions apply, as in 'accelerated depreciation', whereby a firm's total expenditure on plant and equipment may be set against a single year's liability to tax. Selective employment tax, introduced in 1966 to encourage a movement of labour from Britain's service industries into manufacturing, has operated in Northern Ireland very much as in the development areas. Indeed, the Northern Ireland Government has been able to offer some special local concessions. These have been principally outside manufacturing; however, when the premium payment of 38p (90c) per man per week was discontinued in the development areas in April 1970, Northern Ireland's manufacturers continued to enjoy it. This was decided following the 1969 disturbances, as was the introduction for a limited period of a scheme of free compensation for new manufacturing projects against damage arising from riots or civil commotion, including consequential loss. The British system of regional employment premiums, at a rate of £1.50 ($3.60) per man per week to manufacturing industry in the development areas, was also adopted in Northern Ireland in 1967; the British Government agreed to provide the necessary money.

Both the shipbuilding and aircraft industries in Belfast, the city's two largest industrial employers, have received special government aid. Although Harland & Wolff had benefitted from the government's various industrial grants, financial difficulties in the 1960s led to the Shipbuilding Industry (Loans) Act (NI), 1966, which enabled the Ministry of Commerce to lend £3½ million ($8.4 million) 'to facilitate the reorganisation or reconstruction, amalgamation or merger of the company'. In return, the government was empowered to nominate a financial controller. The shipyard also benefitted indirectly from government aid to Belfast harbour commissioners for the construction of a dry dock. It also had access to finance from the Shipbuilding Industry Board, established in 1965 by Westminster legislation; this included an £8 million ($19.2 million) loan towards the construction of a building dock completed in 1970 and designed to accommodate large bulk carriers. The aircraft firm of Short Brothers & Harland has also received aid from both governments; the British Government is actually a majority shareholder. In 1963, provision was made for a grant of £10 million ($24 million), of which the Northern Ireland Government provided one-quarter, so that the firm could complete an order of ten freighters for the Royal Air Force. Further loans from the British Government followed, and in 1969 the Aircraft Industry (Loans) Act (NI), provided for a £3 million ($7.2 million) loan to match a similar loan from the British Government.

The Ministry of Commerce has been the major agency in the new industries drive, but in 1955 the Northern Ireland Development Council was established under the chairmanship of Viscount Chandos. Its headquarters was in London, and the council's role was to publicise the industrial advantages offered by Northern Ireland, to make contact with firms which might consider expanding into Northern Ireland, and to advise the government. The council was wound up at its own request in 1965, after a ten-year period in which close to 30,000 new jobs were created in government-sponsored industry. Its advisory role was to some extent taken over by the Northern Ireland Economic Council, set up in December 1964 to 'consider and recommend on means of furthering the economic development of Northern Ireland with particular reference to the provision of employment, the promotion of economic growth and improved economic efficiency'. This new council had the minister of commerce as chairman, and its members included representatives of both sides of industry. The formation of the council coincided with the publication of Professor Wilson's plan and with a new emphasis on regional planning under a Labour government at Westminster. It was made possible by the solution of a longstanding dispute between the government at Stormont and the trade union movement; the government had hitherto refused to recognise the Northern Ireland Committee of the Dublin-based Irish Congress of Trade Unions, but changed its position after a constitutional change granting more autonomy to the committee. The Economic Council has taken a particular interest in the implementation of the economic plan, and in manpower and industrial training.

It is not easy to measure the success or failure of the government's industrial policies. They have been a success in that industrial production has tended to expand relatively more quickly than in Great Britain, and there has been a substantial diversification of industry, though the concentration of man-made fibres in Northern Ireland in a sense perpetuates the vulnerability of former dependence on the linen industry. The new industries have helped to create a more modern climate of business, and new ideas have been brought in by industrialists from Great Britain, Europe and North America. However, it is arguable that as much might have been achieved had the British Government and the Board of Trade felt a more direct responsibility for industrial development in Northern Ireland; against this, new industrialists frequently express satisfaction with the speed at which it is possible to get decisions from the local ministry. Still, despite the substantial aids to industry, the unemployment problem has remained intractable. The *Northern Ireland Economic Report on 1969*, reviewing the six-year planning period covered by Professor Wilson's report, pointed out that 'In manufacturing industry a total of almost 29,000 new jobs had been created by the end of 1969 compared with the target of 30,000. However the run-down in employment opportunities in the older industries was sufficiently large to offset this, and the net improvement in manufacturing employment was only 5,000 jobs'.

Agriculture

Outside manufacturing industry, a factor in the unemployment figures has been the decline in jobs in agriculture, and by 1970 less than ten per cent of the working population was employed on the land. As the *Northern Ireland Development Programme 1970-75* pointed out, 'The position in agriculture is critical because although subsidies are high the average farmer's income is low. . . . In Great Britain subsidies are equivalent to half of farmers' incomes. In Northern Ireland, however, subsidies are equivalent to virtually the whole of farmers' incomes'. It was estimated in the programme that since 1964 about 3,000 people per year had left farming; of these only 1,250 were retirements or deaths, and the number entering agriculture was estimated to average about 600. By contrast, the census of 1926 indicated that more than one-quarter of the working population was engaged in agriculture.

Farming in Northern Ireland differs in a number of ways from Great Britain, and the existence of the local Ministry of Agriculture has enabled Stormont to introduce policies related to local needs. The average size of farm is smaller than in Great Britain, and there is no tenant-farming. A damper climate imposes greater concentration on grassland and livestock. The Irish Sea imposes additional transport costs on incoming feedingstuffs and outgoing produce, and tends to isolate farmers from their principal market in Great Britain. However, isolation has helped Northern Ireland to deal successfully with such problems as foot-and-mouth disease, brucellosis and plant diseases. As early as 1922, the new parliament passed the Live Stock Breeding Act (NI), requiring that all bulls for breeding be licensed, and it was not until 1931 that Westminster passed a similar measure. One unusual development was that the ministry negotiated an agreement whereby the Queen's University of Belfast established a faculty of agriculture on condition that the government provided the necessary capital grant for buildings and an annual grant for running costs. Members of the faculty are civil

I

servants, whose names are submitted to the university for approval when posts become vacant; they carry out part-time teaching duties, and also undertake research and other duties for the ministry. However, the report of the Lockwood committee on *Higher Education in Northern Ireland* (Cmd 475), published in 1965, recommended ending the arrangement and establishing instead a faculty or school of agriculture at the new university proposed by the committee. This was turned down, in part because of Queen's University's reluctance to lose the faculty, but in the *Northern Ireland Development Programme 1970-75*, the government's consultants said :

> The whole process of re-thinking the future of agriculture in Northern Ireland will be helped if there is available a body of expert agriculturalists, including agricultural economists, who are not closely integrated with the Ministry of Agriculture or closely associated with the provision of educational facilities with which the Ministry is concerned. For this reason we think the time has come for at least some and perhaps all appointments in the Faculty of Agriculture at Queens to be made along normal university lines rather than as joint appointments with the Ministry of Agriculture.

As in industry, there were substantial limitations on the government's powers. However, it was found possible to make important changes in the grading and marketing of produce, beginning with the Marketing of Eggs Act (NI), 1924. Although the Government of Ireland Act, 1920, forbade legislation with regard to trade with any area outside the government's jurisdiction, this could be circumvented by legislation on internal trade. In this instance, wholesale dealers in eggs were required to be licensed by the ministry and to comply with conditions governing the preparation for sale and the consignment of eggs; indirectly, this ensured proper export standards. The anomaly was removed by the Northern Ireland (Miscellaneous Provisions) Act, 1928, and ultimately the government imposed standards on a number of agricultural products. A new phase began when the British Government abandoned free trade in 1931. The Agricultural Marketing Act, 1931, enabled boards to be set up for the marketing of farm produce; the Agricultural Marketing Act

(NI), 1933, was a similar enabling measure, and was followed by schemes for the marketing of pigs, bacon, butter and cream. Northern Ireland did not always follow the British pattern. Since the bulk of pigs were sold for bacon, and there was no alternative market in pork, there was no requirement for pig producers to contract for the supply of pigs to curers; in Great Britain, producers had to supply fixed numbers of pigs on fixed dates. In the case of milk, the majority was for butter manufacture—the reverse of the situation in Great Britain—and this received local assistance through a levy on liquid milk sales and a direct subsidy from the exchequer.

During the 1930s, the British Government became increasingly involved in agricultural questions, and in the regulation of imports and home production. At times it was necessary to decide how Northern Ireland was to benefit from new measures of assistance decided at Westminster, and generally the home secretary became responsible for services which had to be dealt with by Westminster legislation; however, the actual administration was customarily carried out by the Ministry of Agriculture at Stormont, with the cost being borne on the vote of the British Ministry of Agriculture and Fisheries. There was no uniformity in this, however, and the administration of the Wheat Act, 1932, remained with the newly established Wheat Commission. When the Bacon Industry Act, 1938, was introduced the Treasury agreed to similar financial assistance in Northern Ireland; however, local legislation was necessary, and the cost was borne by the local exchequer.

During World War II, the marketing problems of the 1930s disappeared, and emphasis fell on maximum food production. The Ministry of Agriculture acted as agent for a number of British departments, including the new Ministry of Food. In a number of instances, local arrangements differed from the British model; for example, there was a general tillage order requiring a proportion of each farm's arable land to be ploughed, as against the British practice of giving individual cropping directions. The Agriculture Act, 1947, established a system of guaranteed prices and markets for the United Kingdom as a whole, and the relevant part of the Act applied specifically to Northern Ireland; other parts of the Act did not apply, and were paralleled by Stormont legislation. The Agriculture Act, 1957, altered the price support system so that subsidies were related to prices in the market place rather than at the farm gate. This operated to Northern Ireland's disadvantage, and section 32 of the Act provided for a 'remoteness grant' to be paid to the Northern Ireland exchequer. This was originally fixed at £1 million ($2.4 million), but is reviewed every five years, and had risen to £1.75 million ($4.2 million) during 1966-71. The two governments have to reach agreement on the schemes to which the money is devoted; the annual sum is reckoned by the Ministry of Agriculture at Stormont to amount to less than half of the financial disadvantage resulting from remoteness.

When the control of food supplies ended after World War II, the Northern Ireland Government again looked to marketing boards as a means of inducing both stability and quality in farming. The Pigs Marketing Board was reconstituted in 1954, and the Milk Marketing Board followed in 1955. The Seed Potato Marketing Board was set up in 1961, and the Herbage Seed Marketing Board in 1964; the latter was wound up following a decline in production of grass seed. Both the British Egg Marketing Board and the British Wool Board have operated in Northern Ireland as in the rest of the United Kingdom. In addition, a Livestock Marketing Commission was set up in 1967; it is an advisory body only. An Agricultural Trust also began operations in 1967, with the objective of pioneering projects capable of increasing farm incomes.

Transport

Transport is a field in which the Northern Ireland Government has made substantial use of its powers. As early as 1935, it nationalised road transport by purchasing the passenger and freight services operated by private hauliers, and set up the Northern Ireland Road Transport Board; Belfast Corporation, however, continued to operate its own services for local journeys in the city and its outskirts. The purpose of the NIRTB was to ensure co-ordination between road and rail services, and to provide a better service than the private hauliers had done in a very competitive situation. After World War II, the Transport Act (NI), 1948, established the Ulster Transport Authority, which took over the NIRTB's services and also two of the province's three railways. Since the third railway, the Great Northern Railway, operated also in the Republic a separate board was set up in 1953 with representatives of both governments. This arrangement was abandoned in 1958, when the UTA became responsible for the assets and operation of the GNR inside Northern Ireland. For financial reasons, the railways might not have continued to function much longer had they remained in private hands, but the 1948 Act placed on the UTA a duty secure that 'taking one year with another, the revenue of the Authority is not less than sufficient for making provision for the meeting of all charges properly chargeable to revenue'. There was provision for the disposal of property and the closing of lines, and the Transport Act (NI), 1958, virtually imposed on the UTA a duty to terminate rail services which were unlikely to become economic within a reasonable period and which were inconsistent with the authority's obligation to pay its way. The UTA was given until 30 September 1964 to put itself on a sound financial basis, a time limit which was later extended for two years after a reconstruction of its capital in 1962.

Northern Ireland was not unique in finding it difficult to avoid losses on railways, but there were particular problems in the short distances covered and the high mileage of roads; between 1949 and 1967, the number of road vehicles grew from 79,000 to 324,000 while the mileage of railways in service fell from 824 to 200. Nor were the road services always profitable, despite a virtual monopoly; the main exceptions to the monopoly were Belfast's municipal transport, local carriage of goods in Belfast and Londonderry, funerals and furniture removal, and some concessions to farmers. The degree of nationalisation under a Unionist government was greater than under the post-war Labour government in Great Britain, and Northern Ireland did not immediately follow the subsequent Conservative decision to denationalise road services. In a report published in July 1963, *Northern Ireland Railways* (Cmd 458), Mr Henry Benson recommended that the railway system should be reduced to a passenger service for the commuter lines linking Belfast with Bangor, Larne and Portadown, with the line from Portadown to the border being retained to provide a fast rail link between Belfast and Dublin. One of the two lines to Londonderry was subsequently closed, but for political reasons the government was unwilling to sever entirely the rail links between Belfast and Londonderry.

In February 1964, the Minister of Home Affairs, Mr William Craig, announced that the UTA's monopoly of public transport would be abolished. The reorganisation was effected by the Transport Acts (NI), 1966 and 1967, and the UTA was replaced by the Northern Ireland Transport Holding Company, with a number of subsidiary operating companies. The 1966 Act introduced a licensing system for road freight, with licences granted freely to firms which can meet safety and welfare standards; the UTA's services were taken over by Northern Ireland Carriers, a subsidiary jointly owned with the Great Britain Transport Holding Company, and it competes on the same terms as private operators. Ulsterbus was set up to run passenger services, and there was provision for private concerns to provide some services with the holding company's approval; few such services have been undertaken. Northern Ireland Railways took over the rail services, and there was provision for financial assistance from the government and from the profits of the other publicly-owned concerns. The UTA's six hotels were sold to an English hotel group which undertook to modernise them and also to build a new hotel in Belfast. On the whole, the restructuring of public transport has proved a success, and both Ulsterbus and Northern Ireland Carriers have made appreciable profits which have been devoted to re-equipment. Fares and rates have remained comparatively stable. The government's consultants pointed out in their development programme for 1970-5 that the abolition of railways would 'do no more than add a single year's traffic growth to a road system which at present would be well able to accommodate it'.

Should the system be closed or should the Government invest £12-£13 million over the next ten years to preserve the railways in Northern Ireland? It has been suggested that this large sum might be devoted to more worthwhile ventures than maintaining a railway system which will not be economic and which the public only wish to support when it is subsidised. Emotions run high in considering the closure of railway lines but in Londonderry, some local interests indicated that, given a choice, the city would prefer fast and reliable road links to the maintenance of the railway.

The consultants suggested that, provided road communications were improved, it might be possible to close the line to Londonderry during the period of the programme, but the government said it did not propose to close the line during the period. It also considered that 'the present railway system should be given an opportunity to show whether it can provide attractive services at reasonable rates without an excessive amount of financial assistance from the Government'. In 1970, legislation was passed to provide for a further subsidiary company of the Northern Ireland Transport Holding Company, to take over Aldergrove airport near Belfast from the Board of Trade in 1971.

An important factor in the transport field is the government's roads programme. Road transport is virtually the only means of transporting freight, and in 1969 there was one car for every 5.8 persons (against a United Kingdom average of 5.0, and a Scottish average of 6.5). The transport policy statement of February 1964 included a proposal to spend £32 million ($77 million) on motorways and trunk roads, which are now the responsibility of the Ministry of Development. It was calculated that £87 million ($209 million) might be spent on all road projects, including an inner ring motorway in Belfast, during the period 1964-70. In part this was an attempt to channel public resources into an area where rapid expansion seemed possible, and where useful employment would be given, and it was also considered that a well-developed network of roads would be attractive to new industry and help to offset the Irish Sea barrier. In fact, less money was spent than originally planned (even allowing for inflation), but expenditure per head was still half as high again as in Great Britain. Initially, the Ministry of Development envisaged a total expenditure of £142 million ($341 million) during the planning period 1970-5, but this was reduced to £131 million ($314 million) after discussions with the government's consultants, on the grounds that Northern Ireland already enjoyed sufficient advantage over Great Britain in terms of congestion-free roads. It was envisaged that by 1971-2 there would be approximate parity of annual expenditure with Great Britain on a population basis.

Economic and physical planning

Economic planning in Northern Ireland is a comparatively recent development. The first comprehensive study of the economy was commissioned by the Minister of Commerce, Sir Roland Nugent, as unemployment became a serious problem in the 1950s. It was carried out by two Queen's University economists, Professor K. S. Isles and Mr Norman Cuthbert, and submitted in 1955. It presented a gloomy picture, however, and there was some delay before it was published as *An Economic Survey of Northern Ireland* in 1957; it is usually referred to as the Isles report. In 1961, a joint working party of senior officials from relevant United Kingdom and Northern Ireland departments was set up to 'examine and report on the economic situation of Northern Ireland, the factors causing the persistent problem of high unemployment, and the measures that could be taken to bring about a lasting improvement'. Sir Herbert Brittain was appointed chairman, and he was succeeded on his death by Sir Robert Hall.

The *Report of the Joint Working Party on the Economy of Northern Ireland* (Cmd 446), commonly known as the Hall report, was published in October 1962 and offered no real hope of solving the unemployment problem. The working party was unable to reach agreement on a proposal by the Northern Ireland Government to introduce an 'employment subsidy', envisaged as a grant of 50p ($1.20) per week for adult employees in productive industry. Its opponents argued that

> By maintaining employment (especially of scarce skilled labour) in existing industries which cannot be expected to expand it would, on this view, prevent the labour becoming available for new growth industries and thereby inhibit the healthy process of change and development. Secondly, it would be difficult to discontinue the subsidy, once introduced, while the difficulties of the old staple industries might well lead to pressure to increase it.

In essence, the proposed subsidy was identical to the regional employment premiums introduced by the Labour government in Great Britain in 1967. Apart from recommending an expanded housing programme, the working party turned down any general expansion of the public works programme :

> In our analysis of the economic situation we reached the conclusion . . . that, since the region was far from self-sufficient, additional employment could only be created either by increased exports or by increased subventions from Great Britain. Public works must depend on the latter though these may be offset by savings in unemployment benefit and assistance payments. They may strengthen the economy and enable it to export more, but most of them are a very indirect means of doing this. The case for an increase in public works on general economic grounds does not, therefore, seem strong.

The working party added that the encouragement of migration, either to Great Britain or elsewhere, should be regarded as 'one of a composite mixture of measures to alleviate unemployment, and further steps should be taken to find employment opportunities outside Northern Ireland and to induce unemployed workers to avail themselves of them'. The popular view of the Hall report was that it was a failure, offering nothing better than emigration as a cure for unemployment.

Capt Terence O'Neill brought a new optimism to the problems when he became prime minister in 1963, and he immediately commissioned an economic plan from Professor Wilson. The Wilson plan, published in 1965, called for 'an environment more favourable to the sustained expansion of output and employment'. It listed a number of growth centres capable of sustaining industrial development, and laid emphasis on training facilities to provide a pool of skilled labour. A target of 12,000 new houses a year by 1970 was set; this compared with a target of 10,000 houses in the Hall report and an actual output which had gone as low as 4,894 in 1959 and recovered to 8,215 in 1962. (The Hall target was reached in 1966, and the Wilson target in 1968.) The plan set three employment targets : 30,000 new jobs in manufacturing industry; a programme of public and private investment likely to provide 5,000 additional jobs in the construction industry; an additional 30,000 jobs in the service industries, an estimate based on the existing rate of expansion.

> With so many uncertainties, it is clearly impossible to make a precise estimate of the number of new jobs needed in order to achieve full employment in Northern Ireland. Superficially at least, the problem would be easier if it were possible to assign one of those now unemployed to each new vacancy as it appeared but it would, of course, be fanciful to suppose that the labour market could, or should, be made to operate in this way. In fact it must be anticipated that a large proportion of any new vacancies will be offset in various other ways: by the natural increase in the adult popula- tions, by the decline in the net migration that may be anticipated when there are additional openings at home, by a rise in the participation rate that is likely to occur for the same reason, by the continuing movement of people out of agriculture and from those manufacturing firms that are contracting employment.

The employment target in the construction industry was reached in 1968. The target for manufacturing industry was largely achieved, but very largely offset by the contraction and closure of existing firms. In the service industries, there were only 11,600 extra jobs by the end of 1969. However, in manufacturing industry, there was a comparatively sharp increase in the proportion of male workers; having risen only $1\frac{1}{2}$ per cent between 1950 and 1964, it rose another three per cent to fifty-nine per cent in 1968. The 1970 development programme included an analysis of the growth of the insured population between 1960 and 1968. The actual growth was from 482,000 employees to 515,000 employees; however, had the various industrial classifications grown or contracted at the same rates as in Great Britain, the 1968 figure would only have been 501,000. 'The moral is clear : if Northern Ireland can maintain these faster growth rates in the years ahead and if major adjustments such as the decline in shipbuilding employment are no longer required on the same scale, then faster employment growth will be possible in the future.'

Professor Wilson's economic plan was preceeded by a major exercise in physical planning. Its author was Professor Sir Robert Matthew, and his *Belfast Regional Survey and Plan: Recommendations and Conclusions* (Cmd 451) was published in February 1963. An interim report, designating a number of housing sites for Belfast Corporation, was published in January 1961. The full regional survey and plan was published in April 1964. Professor Matthew drew attention to the deficiencies in planning legislation :

> It was not until 1931 that Northern Ireland had any Statute Law on Town and Country Planning. The idea of the 'Statutory Planning Scheme', under the 1931 Planning and Housing Act, failed. Making of schemes was not obligatory, and none were, in fact, confirmed. Up to the War, it could be said with truth that development in every field was unplanned. The Planning (Interim Development) Act of 1944 'deemed' that a Resolution to prepare a Planning Scheme had been passed for every area in the country. Since then, a permanent 'Interim' planning situation has been allowed to develop, pending the emergence of a 'Planning Scheme'. No planning schemes have been completed, and it would appear that the existing legislation is a dead letter.

Two provisions in the Government of Ireland Act, 1920, had presented difficulties : the prohibition on taking property without compensation, and the absolute prohibition on compulsory acquisition of church property except for roads, railways and various public utilities. In December 1959, a House of Lords judgement in the case of O. D. Cars Ltd *v* Belfast Corporation upheld a provision in the 1931 Act that no compensation need be paid in respect of certain planning provisions considered reasonable by the responsible ministry. The Northern Ireland Act, 1962, removed the prohibition on taking property without compensation; it also made possible the compulsory acquisition of certain church property for housing, slum clearance, development and redevelopment.

The Matthew plan was not the first venture of its kind. In August 1942, the government had set up a Planning Commission. It was composed of technical officers representing government departments and local authorities, and it produced reports on *Planning Proposals for the Belfast Area* in 1945 and 1952 (Cmd 227 and 302) and on *Location of Industry in Northern Ireland* (Cmd 225). A broadly based Planning Advisory Board was set up in September 1942; its most notable report was on *The Ulster Countryside*, published in 1947. However, the will to take effective action was lacking in the immediate post-war period, and Professor Matthew was able to comment :

> Over all, the quality of environment, the most powerful aid to prosperity in the modern world, has been neglected, and is visibly deteriorating. Public opinion, it is true, is awakening, but only slowly; meanwhile, the situation as development increases and pressures on land increase is reaching a critical stage. Progressively, the cost of repairing the damage becomes heavier and the point of no return may be within sight. This would be disastrous for the future of Northern Ireland, in a world where competition for good environments is rapidly becoming a real factor in the balance-sheet of material well-being.

Faced with congestion in Belfast, a heavy backlog of slum clearance and an inadequate supply of land for redevelopment, Professor Matthew aimed 'simultaneously to *de-magnetize the centre,* and re-invigorate the many attractive small towns in the region'. The most dramatic proposal was to link the towns of Portadown and Lurgan in county Armagh to form a new city, subsequently called Craigavon; this envisaged a population increase of 64,000 in 1961-81 to a total of 100,000. Seven other growth centres were named, again with a population increase of 64,000, while the Belfast urban area was to increase from 560,000 to only 600,000. To curb Belfast's growth, the plan limited the area available for housing; the boundary is known as the Matthew stop-line. Professor Matthew recommended that the responsibility for planning should rest directly with the government, acting through a minister for planning and development.

The government accepted the Matthew strategy, and it was endorsed also in the Wilson plan. In March 1964, the government published a White Paper on *The Administration of Town and Country Planning in Northern Ireland* (Cmd 465), in which it proposed a central planning authority, directly responsible to the Minister of Health and Local Government, to take over all planning powers and duties. However, local authorities were reluctant to lose their planning powers, and the issue had not been resolved when in 1970 the review body on local government recommended that planning powers be vested directly in the Ministry of Development (established on 1 January 1965). However, the New Towns Act (NI), 1965, provided for the creation of the Craigavon Development Commission, and the government accepted full responsibility for the payment of compensation under the Planning Acts in the Land Development Values (Compensation) Act (NI), 1965. The Amenity Lands Act (NI), 1965, provided important new powers to protect areas of visual beauty or scientific interest. Under the Act, the ministry is advised by the Ulster Country-side Committee and the Nature Reserves Committee. The designation of an area of outstanding natural beauty means that the local planning authority must consult the Ulster Countryside Committee before reaching a decision on any planning applications; among the first areas designated were the Lagan valley, the Antrim coast and glens, and the Mourne mountains. There are also powers to designate extensive areas of countryside as national parks, with a park committee as planning authority for the area and with wardens to advise both landowners and visitors. The ministry also has power to safeguard smaller areas of natural beauty and amenity by taking them into public ownership or by negotiating restrictive covenants with landowners; similar provisions exist for nature reserves, and in areas of scientific interest the planning authority is required to consult the Nature Reserves Committee about applications for development.

The *Northern Ireland Development Programme 1970-75* combined economic and physical planning. Its authors were Professors Wilson and Matthew, together with Professor Jack Parkinson, a former Queen's University economist who had helped Wilson with the earlier plan. An introductory survey begins by posing the question 'Is Northern Ireland viable?' and points out that, despite a long record of practical action by the government, unemployment stood at 6.8 per cent at mid-1969 compared with 2.2 per cent for the whole United Kingdom, while output per head of working population had been running at about seventy-five per cent of the national average. The consultants warned of the effect of civil disorders on industrial development, and noted that they had been 'much concerned about the danger that Northern Ireland may be caught in a vicious circle of political instability and industrial decline'. The consultants were advised early in their inquiry that 40,000 new jobs in manufacturing industry might be promoted during 1970-5; this had been deemed the minimum desirable, but after the disorders 'has now the appearance of presenting an immensely formidable task'.

The consultants took the view that, in the absence of an industrial national plan, 'an indicative plan with quantitative targets for output, employment and investment industry by industry cannot be prepared'. Their programme for action was consequently limited in scope, and had four main features : making the general environment still more favourable to expansion, continuing with an active policy of industrial promotion, improving the physical environment as a direct contribution to the standard of living, and planning the government's own activities to ensure consistency and assess what was involved in money and manpower. An accompanying government statement (Cmd 547) accepted the broad outlines of the consultants' programme, and announced an extension of the range of incentives to industry. These included capital grants within the range of forty-five to sixty per cent, depending on the location and employment offered; the West and South East were singled out as areas where worthwhile projects would attract the maximum rate of grant. More generous loans were to be made available, together with special aid to ease the financial burdens of key personnel moving to any part of Northern Ireland and 'employment grants' to help firms meet the initial costs of establishing new projects. The government decided also to establish a 'local enterprise development unit', based on the Ministry of Commerce, to stimulate local initiative, particularly in places which as a rule had proved too small or too remote to attract incoming industry.

The consultants largely endorsed existing policy in physical planning, but pointed out that 'Statutory powers and administrative machinery are gravely inadequate for the implementation of the policies to which Government is committed'. The major failure had been to contain the growth of the Belfast urban area, which by 1970 had almost reached the 1981 target of 600,000 people. Despite the preparation of area and transport plans by the city's own consultants, the redevelopment of Belfast had gone slowly and was being made more difficult by the shortage of land; thus, the 1970-5 programme provided for some breaches of the Matthew stop-line. By contrast, Craigavon had grown less rapidly than anticipated, and some industries found difficulty recruiting labour. On the other hand, Antrim had grown very rapidly; the consultants estimated a 1975 population of 22,000-24,000 compared with Matthew's original 1981 target of 12,000. The 1970-5 programme envisaged a future city region, the Greater Belfast Area, based on a triangle formed by Belfast, Antrim and Craigavon. This area and Londonderry were to be heavily orientated towards the accommodation of major industrial projects, with the forward provision of infrastructure for this and for anticipated population growth. Both Belfast and Londonderry, cities affected by civil disturbances, were to enjoy special measures to improve social conditions. Other 'accelerated industrial growth' was to be concentrated on Ballymena and eight other 'key centres'. The government accepted the consultant's proposal to set up a 'central mobility office' in Belfast, providing financial incentives to encourage people to move to different parts of Northern Ireland.

The development programme envisaged public expenditure averaging £480 million ($1,152 million) per year during 1970-5. Most of this had been anticipated before the programme was published, but a number of changes (notably in industrial incentives and the housing programme) added £74 million ($178 million) to the five-year total. The government statement noted that 'the United Kingdom Government has agreed that, subject to any adjustment which might from time to time be required in connection with the task of managing the economy as a whole, additional finance will be made available where necessary to implement the Programme'. However, a local contribution was made in that the government announced that in 1971 it would withdraw an estate duty concession affecting the middle range of estates (introduced to help family firms), and in 1972 reduce industrial derating from seventy-five to fifty per cent.

Housing

Housing is an area in which the Northern Ireland

Government has been able to introduce policies devised to meet local needs. Since the passing of the Housing Act (NI), 1945, the government has been trying to make good the neglect of the inter-war years, when only some 50,000 houses were built. In this period, there was provision for state assistance for the construction of houses for workers in urban areas, and of cottages for agricultural workers in rural areas. During 1919-39, local authorities built 3,839 houses and private builders 32,644 houses with state aid; 3,669 labourers' cottages were built. About 10,000 more houses were built without state assistance. There was a much higher ratio of old houses to new than in Great Britain, and house-building virtually halted during the war years. In 1944, a committee of the Planning Advisory Board concluded that 100,000 new houses were required with a minimum of delay, and that a complete programme of slum clearance and the ending of overcrowding would require at least 200,000 houses. At that time, Northern Ireland had 323,000 houses.

The Housing Act (NI), 1944, provided for the payment of lump sum subsidies to local authorities erecting houses. Then, following the establishment of the Ministry of Health and Local Government in 1944, the 1945 Act established a single code for subsidy payments in rural and urban areas; the state provided annual contributions for forty years in respect of each new local authority house, while the local authorities contributed fixed sums from the rates over the same period, which in 1946 was increased to sixty years. The 1945 Act also set up the Northern Ireland Housing Trust, a public authority empowered to erect houses throughout Northern Ireland. Its role was to supplement the effort of local authorities; its houses attracted the same level of subsidy, but the full amount was paid by the government, except where (infrequently) the trust acted as an agent of the local authority. Thus, while it had been government policy between the wars to encourage private rather than public building— though with less generous aid than was available in Great Britain—there was a new emphasis on public housing. The level of subsidies was more generous than in Great Britain— the 'leeway' agreement was at work—and Northern Ireland became the only part of the United Kingdom to offer subsidies for private enterprise building. The Housing and Local Government (Miscellaneous Provisions) Act (NI), 1946, provided subsidies for houses built for private letting, but there was little incentive to compete with public authority housing. However, the Housing (No. 2) Act (NI), 1946, provided subsidies for houses built privately for sale or occupation, and additional provisions for farmers and their employees were contained in the Housing on Farms Acts (NI), 1948 and 1950.

With variations in interest rates and in the level of subsidies, the rate of house-building fluctuated from year to year. The number of completions fell from 8,399 in 1952 to 4,894 in 1959. The government subsequently worked out a system whereby the levels of subsidy were altered to take account of changes in building costs or the interest rates charged by the government loans fund. The purpose was to encourage housing authorities to maintain a steady building programme, and by 1968 the number of completions was 12,120. By the end of 1969, the total of post-war housing was 176,086. These included 66,828 dwellings built by local authorities; 42,160 by the Housing Trust; 4,042 by other public agencies, including housing associations; 55,167 by private enterprise with subsidy; 7,306 by private enterprise without subsidy; and 583 rebuilt war-destroyed houses. The contribution of the Housing Trust is measured not only in numbers of dwellings. As the largest single house-building agency—its members are appointed by the minister of development—it has provided more attractive estates than most of the smaller local authorities have done, and has put more emphasis on the training of housing managers.

The Housing (Miscellaneous Provisions) and Rent Restriction Law (Amendment) Act (NI), 1956, contained important provisions dealing with slum clearance and redevelopment. All housing authorities were required to submit to the Ministry of Health and Local Government within two years their proposals for dealing with unfit houses. The Act set out the conditions for recognising redevelopment areas, and provided for fifty per cent grants to local authorities in respect of spending on redevelopment. Land purchased for use as open space attracted a seventy-five per cent grant. The Act also

K

enabled local authorities to pay grants towards the conversion or improvement of housing. The local authorities' subsequent survey indicated that some 50,000 houses were totally unfit for human habitation, and another 40,000 unfit but capable of repair. The Housing Act (NI), 1961, provided for additional payments to relieve hardship resulting from slum clearance. These covered houses which were well maintained, or were used for business, or were occupied by the owner; resettlement grants were also made. The 1961 Act extended to the Housing Trust the government grants that had previously been available only to local authorities.

The report of the Cameron Commission on *Disturbances in Northern Ireland* (Cmd 532), published in September 1969, pointed to

> A rising sense of continuing injustice and grievance among large sections of the Catholic population in Northern Ireland, in particular in Londonderry and Dungannon, in respect of (i) inadequacy of housing provision by certain local authorities (ii) unfair methods of allocation of houses built and let by such authorities, in particular, refusals and omissions to adopt a 'points' system in determining priorities and making allocations (iii) misuse in certain cases of discretionary powers of allocation of houses in order to perpetuate Unionist control of the local authority.

The commission noted that there was frequently a 'gentleman's agreement' whereby houses in Catholic wards would be allocated to Catholics by Catholic councillors, with a converse allocation in Protestant wards. 'Such practices at one time were accepted by almost all shades of opinion as representing a compromise way of life, but it is clear from the evidence we have heard that they are now increasingly felt to be open to objection as operating unjustly and tending to perpetuate rather than to heal or eliminate sectarian divisions.'

The reform programme of 22 November 1968 included a commitment to ensure that all housing authorities placed need in the forefront when allocating houses, and that future allocations would be carried out on the basis of a readily understood and published scheme. The Ministry of Development subsequently prepared a model scheme for allocating houses, and local authorities were required to introduce this 'group plus points' system or an agreed alternative. The scheme provided for housing authorities to divide applicants into six separate groups. Three groups—those displaced by slum clearance or public works, incoming workers and emergency cases—did not require points. The others were elderly persons, applicants sharing accommodation or in overcrowded conditions, and medical cases. However, there was provision for the centralisation of public housing in legislation introduced in July 1970, following the inter-governmental discussions of October 1969. The Housing Executive Bill (NI), 1970, provided for a Northern Ireland Housing Executive with a consultative and advisory Housing Council drawn from each of the housing authorities. Three of the nine members of the executive were to be nominated by the council from its members, with the minister of development selecting the other six and nominating the chairman. The Bill provided for a phased transfer of housing, with local authorities and the Housing Trust first acting as agents of the executive; the executive would later take over directly, and later still assume the housing functions of the development commissions in Craigavon, Antrim-Ballymena and Londonderry.

Health and welfare

The health and welfare services provide a similar story of attempts to make good the deficiencies of the inter-war years. In 1921, the new government had inherited services markedly inferior to those in Great Britain. Many of the hospitals were workhouse infirmaries provided under the poor law, and the poor law guardians also employed dispensary medical officers and midwives to cater for the needy and destitute. Local authority services were poorly developed in respect of maternity and child care and the prevention of tuberculosis, and the mortality rate was higher than in other parts of the United Kingdom. Overall responsibility rested with the Ministry of Home Affairs, and its first minister, Sir Dawson Bates, set on foot a departmental inquiry into local government. A report published in 1927 (Cmd 73) proposed substantial reforms which included the establishment of county health committees, the abolition of boards of guardians, the closing of workhouses and an expansion of hospital facilities. However, the government was hard pressed for finance, and it was not until the Ministry of Health and Local Government was established in 1944 that a real transformation occurred. Still, the inter-war years did see the construction of two large maternity hospitals and a hospital for sick children in Belfast. A number of union infirmaries were converted into district hospitals which could accept fee-paying patients. However, these hospitals put a burden on the rates and (because of derating) on the exchequer, and conversion was eventually discouraged by the minister. In 1939, there were twelve district hospitals, six county infirmaries, twelve union infirmaries, and a small number of voluntary hospitals. The National Health Insurance Act (NI), 1930, had introduced free general practitioner treatment for insured persons; the original National Insurance Act, 1911, had provided cash benefits during illness but had not extended medical benefit to Ireland.

The creation of a separate ministry was recommended by a select committee in 1944 (HC 601), and there were other proposals similar to those made in 1927. The first minister was Mr William Grant, a former shipyard worker and member of the Ulster Unionist Labour Association, and he quickly brought forward legislative reforms. The Public Health and Local Government (Administrative Provisions) Act (NI), 1946, provided for statutory health committees in each county and county borough, and these gradually assumed the powers and duties of urban and district councils and of the boards of guardians. In addition, county welfare committees were also set up. The Public Health (Tuberculosis) Act (NI), 1946, set up the Northern Ireland Tuberculosis Authority to tackle a problem of particular severity. Finally, the Health Services Act (NI), 1948, introduced free and comprehensive medical treatment on the same general lines as the new British system, but with the creation of two new statutory bodies, the Northern Ireland Hospitals Authority and the General Health Services Board.

The tuberculosis authority, NITA, was composed of thirteen members nominated by the county and county borough councils, and four nominated by the minister, with power to co-opt two others. It took over the functions of the counties in respect of institutional and domiciliary treatment of tuberculosis. In 1946, the death-rate from tuberculosis was 83 per 100,000; in 1957, it was 12.5 per 100,000, and there were vacant beds in chest hospitals. At this point, a joint committee of NITA and the Hospitals Authority was set up, and its report led to a merger under the Health Services Act (NI), 1958, with the domiciliary functions going to the county health and welfare authorities. The precedent set by NITA was followed when the Hospitals Authority was set up in 1948, and the new authority enjoyed greater independence than regional hospital boards in Great Britain. One indication of this was that hospitals taken over under the Act were vested in the authority and not in the minister. Similarly, while the Westminster legislation charged the minister with the duty of providing the necessary hospital services through the agency of the regional board, the minister of health and local government in Northern Ireland was only required to 'promote' the provision of health services in general and to secure the effective co-ordination of the various services. There was, of course, a financial control and the minister appointed the members of the authority (subject to certain provisions about consultation and ultimate composition), but the lack of full ministerial responsibility meant that MPs could not always get answers to parliamentary questions about hospitals administration. Although the authority embarked on a substantial programme of modernisation and extension—provision for 'leeway' meant higher capital expenditure per head of population than in Great Britain—it was criticised for being bureaucratic and inefficient. The General Health Services Board was similarly criticised, though its independent status was probably less significant in practical terms.

The *Report of the Committee on the Health Services in Northern Ireland* (Cmd 334) pointed to the anomaly that

> final responsibility for expenditure should rest with one body and responsibility for the policy which largely determines expenditure with another . . . .
>
> Just as responsibility for detailed planning and executive action should lie with one body, so in our opinion responsibility at the highest level for finance and policy must rest with

the Ministry. We subscribe to the principle that a service which is financed entirely from voted moneys must be subject finally to Parliamentary, and therefore to Ministerial, control; and we see no alternative to this which does not infringe constitutional practice and precedent and contain inherent possibilities of friction and confusion.

The committee, under Dr H. G. Tanner, recommended that both the Hospitals Authority and the General Health Services Board should become agents of the ministry. This was rejected by the minister, Dame Dehra Parker, but pressure continued and under the Health Services (Amendment) Act (NI), 1967, the authority became an agent of the Ministry of Health and Social Services. The General Health Services Board retained its direct responsibility for providing general medical, dental, pharmaceutical and ophthalmic services. The board is not unlike the British executive councils, but—being one body compared with more than one hundred in Great Britain—has been able to carry out more extensive functions, such as the control of admissions to vacancies in general medical practice and the work carried out by dental estimates committees and drug-pricing bureaux in Great Britain.

The Hospitals Authority has also undertaken functions not exercised by regional hospital boards in Great Britain; these include the ambulance service (health authorities in Great Britain) and the administration of teaching hospitals (in England and Wales, boards of governors are directly responsible to Whitehall). The authority also provides a comprehensive system of care for the mentally subnormal; this includes not only institutional care but also community care, which in Great Britain has been the responsibility of local health and welfare authorities. The Health Services Act (NI), 1948, transferred to the Hospitals Authority the six existing mental hospitals which had hitherto been vested in county and county borough councils. The Mental Health Act (NI), 1948, provided for the first time a code of law for the ascertainment, care, supervision, training and occupation of 'persons requiring special care'. The Mental Health Act (NI), 1961, further reformed the law so as to integrate psychiatry more closely with other branches of medicine and to provide for the treatment of mental illness on lines (administratively speaking) similar to the treatment of physical illness. A new term, 'mental disorder', was introduced to cover all forms of mental illness or handicap.

In July 1969, the government published a Green Paper on *The Administrative Structure of the Health and Personal Social Services in Northern Ireland* as a basis for public discussion and consultation with representative bodies. It proposed to abolish the tripartite structure of Hospitals Authority, General Health Services Board and county health committees, and to substitute a maximum of five area boards responsible as agents of the ministry for providing health and possibly welfare services. The boards would have twenty to twenty-four members nominated by the minister after appropriate consultation with local authority and professional interests.

The case for an integrated structure might be summed up as follows:—

(a) the present structure is tripartite while the individual's needs for services should be seen as a continuum;

(b) the separate branches of the health services are increasingly interdependent in treatment and care, and the administrative structure should be designed to secure fully co-ordinated planning as well as joint action;

(c) a single authority for each area could more easily secure the most effective use of the financial and human resources available;

(d) advances in knowledge and the emergence of new needs make it desirable that resources can be quickly and effectively deployed to meet new situations;

(e) the different financial basis of the local authority services has presented obstacles to the balanced development of community care;

(f) the three-tier management structure in the hospital service [ministry, Hospitals Authority and hospital management committees] leads to duplication of effort and difficulties in communication.

The Green Paper noted that a single board for the whole of Northern Ireland would seem to have 'the virtues of simplicity, of ensuring consistency and of providing a base for services which would continue to need to be given on a Provincial basis', but argued that this would deprive local interests of an adequate part in determining the provision of services in their area and could lose touch with local needs. The report of the review body on local government (Cmd 546), published in June 1970, largely endorsed the Green Paper's proposals. It took the view that personal health and welfare services should be the direct responsibility of the Ministry of Health and Social Services. The review body concluded that autonomous bodies were not in general appropriate for services which carried social implications; it pointed to insulation against pressure of public opinion, to the difficult and delicate relationship between ministry and board, and to problems of accountability to Parliament. The report envisaged four area boards which would clearly be agents of the ministry and which would include a proportion of local authority representatives.

Education

In education, too, there has been a need to make good the neglect of the inter-war years. The post-war pattern was set by a White Paper on *Educational Reconstruction in Northern Ireland* (Cmd 226), published in December 1944, and the subsequent Education Act (NI), 1947. The pattern broadly follows the British model, and the major variations are a product of history and (see chapter 4) Northern Ireland's plural society. The minister of education can draw on the advice of an Advisory Council for Education, which at different times has been asked to consider such issues as the selection of pupils for different types of secondary education, the age of transfer of these pupils, arrangements for children requiring special educational treatment, and the supply of and demand for teachers. The Youth and Sports Council for Northern Ireland also advises the minister on certain matters, and there are a number of standing committees on such matters as curricula and teachers' salaries.

In 1964, a White Paper on *Educational Development in Northern Ireland* (Cmd 470) afforded an opportunity to review progress and set new targets. Some of these were physical targets : the replacement of many unsatisfactory primary school buildings, the closure of small rural schools, and the reduction of the size of classes. Of the 1,482 primary schools operating on 31 March 1963, half had been built before 1900. More than 300 schools had no piped water supply, more than 850 had no central heating, and more than 450 had no form of artificial lighting. Out of 6,007 primary classes in January 1963, fully 1,045 had more than forty children. However, the most persistent educational controversy had been on the method of selection for different types of secondary education and (to a lesser extent) on whether segregation according to presumed ability and aptitude was desirable. The White Paper examined the arguments for and against comprehensive education, and concluded :

> . . . even if the Government took full powers to reconstruct the secondary school system on comprehensive lines irrespective of established interests or opinions, the actual size and location of many existing school premises would present formidable difficulties.
>
> Such a proposal would moreover be certain to arouse strong opposition. Some voluntary grammar schools might, indeed, claim the right to secede from the grant-aided educational system and to operate as independent schools wholly dependent on fees, which would of course have to be very much higher than they are now. This would set up a social cleavage within the Northern Ireland educational system such as it has never known before.
>
> Given, therefore, the facts of the existing situation and the disruption, expense, restriction of parental choice and ill-feeling which would be caused by an imposed system of comprehensive schools, the Government is satisfied that it would be wrong to make a complete change in the pattern of secondary education established under the 1947 Act.

The government's compromise was to encourage experiments in secondary school organisation designed to reduce the importance of selection at the age of eleven-plus; this included a promise to 'consider sympathetically agreements reached locally to reorganise the secondary schools of an area on a non-selective basis and proposals to establish in developing areas non-selective secondary schools'. Intermediate schools were renamed secondary (intermediate) schools, and steps were taken to lessen the differences between them and grammar schools. These included the adoption of a common formula for determining numbers of staff in a school, and the promotion of academic streams and extended courses where practicable. Indeed, some experiments had already occurred in the smaller provincial towns which had not enough 'qualified' pupils to support a grammar school of adequate size; these either meant the conversion of an existing small grammar school to a 'bilateral secondary school' or the provision of academic courses in new intermediate schools. Some intermediate schools in Belfast had also enhanced their prestige by introducing academic courses leading to the General Certificate of Education, often achieving results which cast doubt on the validity of selection at eleven-plus. Down County Education Committee later built two new comprehensive 'high schools' at Dundonald, an area of rapid population growth on the outskirts of Belfast.

One effect of the government's policy was that Northern Ireland avoided the bitter local controversies which accompanied the attempts of the 1964-70 Labour government to impose comprehensive education in Great Britain. Whether it was an educationally satisfactory policy is another question, and it appeared likely that educationists would increasingly press for the adaptation of existing schools to some form of comprehensive education. Meanwhile, the 1964 White Paper announced the discontinuation of the qualifying examination in its existing form. There had already been modifications— the arithmetic and English papers had been shortened, and children were allowed to take the examination in their own schools—and there later emerged a system of verbal reasoning tests allied to teachers' assessments of their own pupils. However, there continued to be criticisms, and the stigma of failure attached to more than three-quarters of the entrants. There were anomalies in that local education authorities had discretion to declare qualified between twenty-five and seventy-five per cent of border-line cases, and the outcome depended on the number of grammar school places available in the county.

There has been a steady expansion in post-secondary education in recent years. The most notable features have been the establishment of the New University of Ulster at Coleraine, county Londonderry, and the setting up of an Ulster College with constituent colleges in such fields as technology, commerce and management, physical education, art and domestic science. Both follow recommendations of the report on *Higher Education in Northern Ireland* (Cmd 475), prepared by a committee under Sir John Lockwood and published in 1965. The committee's choice of Coleraine as the site of Northern Ireland's second university was severely criticised in Londonderry, where it had been hoped that the existing Magee University College (originally a Presbyterian institution) would form the nucleus of a new university. As the Cameron Commission later pointed out, this 'caused a degree of unity in resentment and protest which was probably unique, at least in the recent history of the city, and united local opinion in a suspicion that the central government was deliberately discriminating against the city and its interests for political reasons'. The discontent of this period, expressed in the 'University for Derry' campaign, was a contributory factor in the emergence of the city's civil rights movement.

The quality of life

The post-war years have seen increasing government efforts to improve the quality of Ulster life. There have been increasing grants to the Arts Council of Northern Ireland, which was originally established in 1943 as the Council for the Encouragement of Music and the Arts. It is governed by a board which is partly nominated by the minister of education and by the senate of the Queen's University of Belfast, and partly elected by associates of the council. The council has probably been most successful in encouraging painting and music—though the Ulster Orchestra formed in 1966 has proved a drain on its resources—and least successful in encouraging Ulster writing or raising the standards of local theatre. The Ulster Museum, formerly a municipal institution in Belfast, became a national museum under 1961 legislation. The Ulster Folk Museum at Cultra, county Down, was established under 1958 legislation and opened in 1964; three years later, legislation provided for the Belfast Transport Museum to be moved to Cultra. The Public Record Office's collection of historic material is growing steadily, and the office now publishes a sizeable number of historical studies. The Ministry of Finance maintains a number of ancient monuments, and oversees others considered worthy of preservation; a survey of industrial archaeology has been completed. Much of the work of preserving beauty spots and buildings of architectural or historic interest has been undertaken by the National Trust. A local committee of the trust was first formed in 1937, and there has been generous assistance from the Ulster Land Fund, set up in 1948 with a capital of £1 million ($2.4 million) with objectives of this sort. The government also provides grants for Armagh observatory, founded in 1790; a planetarium was opened in the observatory grounds in 1968. The expansion of facilities for sport is encouraged by the Ministry of Education, and a Youth and Sports Council advises on grants which should be given to voluntary organisations and public bodies.

The development programme for 1970-5 envisaged special intention to public investment and other measures designed to improve social conditions in Belfast and Londonderry; these two cities were to be the main beneficiaries of a £6 million ($14.4 million) programme drawn up by the ministries of Education and Development, and of the £1 million made available to the Ministry of Community Relations to administer the Social Need (Grants) Act (NI), 1970, in urban areas of deprivation. The development programme also contained an urban and rural improvement campaign, with labour-intensive schemes to enhance amenity and encourage tourism. The Northern Ireland Tourist Board was established by statute in 1948 and, while its principal objective is to attract holidaymakers from other areas, the government statement on the development programme noted it was 'a legitimate object of tourist policy to encourage Northern Ireland residents to holiday within the country'.

Clearly, as Northern Ireland neared the completion of fifty years of self-government, great economic and social advances were still needed. In some areas, Northern Ireland still fell far short of British standards, and in almost every area the degree of progress had depended very much on the available government finance. Further progress was threatened by civil disorder; generous financial assistance from the British Government was likely to accomplish less than it might have done in earlier, more peaceful times.

6

Relations with Westminster

In *The Government of Northern Ireland*, Nicholas Mansergh criticised strongly the financial relationship between Northern Ireland and Great Britain.

> . . . even though one allows the economic problems of the six counties to be naturally greater in intensity than those of Great Britain as a whole, that does not justify the present financial relationship. For it is its weakness that in its day to day application it adheres to no clearly-defined principle; and that it carries no conviction of an ability to secure a just distribution of financial burdens.
>
> The Imperial Government has displayed no little anxiety lest any public discussion on any aspect of the relationship between Great Britain and Northern Ireland should reopen the Irish Question as a whole. This anxiety is shared by the Government of Northern Ireland. Yet a critical analysis of the financial system now in force is needed either to restore public confidence in its equity or to confirm public suspicion of its inherent incapacity to secure a proper distribution of revenue and expenditure as between the two parts of the United Kingdom. Moreover, the present system labours under two particular disadvantages. On the one hand its operation is totally incomprehensible to the general public; on the other, the widest discretion in determining all outstanding questions is vested in a non-democratic body whose deliberations and whose proceedings are secret.

What was true in 1936 is true today, though it is apparent that the British Government treats Northern Ireland much more generously than when Mansergh was writing. The history of Northern Ireland's financial relations with Great Britain has been one of evading the consequences of the Government of Ireland Act, 1920. Over the fifty years of self-government,

Northern Ireland has increasingly sacrificed its financial independence (and with it much legislative and administrative independence) in return for more and more financial assistance from the British exchequer.

The anomaly of the 1920 Act was to make Northern Ireland a separate financial region, self-financing and with its revenues separated from the national accounts, but at the same time to deny it the power to raise whatever revenues were necessary for the proper government of the area. Even at the beginning, some eighty-eight per cent of Northern Ireland's revenue was levied by the British Government, and 'transferred revenue' raised by local taxes has always been a small proportion of the total. Reserved taxes include customs and excise duties, income tax and supertax, and various profits taxes. From these are deducted the cost of operating reserved services in Northern Ireland; these include the inland revenue and customs and excise departments, the Supreme Court, the Post Office and the British Broadcasting Corporation. A further deduction, known as the imperial contribution, is made towards the cost of the armed services, defence and matters arising from war, the national debt and a number of other items falling on the British exchequer. The 'residuary share of reserved revenue' is then transferred to the Northern Ireland exchequer. Taxes transferred to the Northern Ireland Parliament include death duties, stamp duties, entertainments duty and motor vehicle duty. Responsibility for the allocation of the reserved revenue rests with a statutory Joint Exchequer Board, consisting of representatives of the Treasury and the Ministry of Finance, with a chairman appointed by the Crown; in practice, this is likely to mean approving a division of revenue already agreed by Stormont and Whitehall, and there have been long periods when the board has not met. The board, which is Mansergh's 'non-democratic body whose deliberations and whose proceedings are secret', can arbitrate in other issues arising from the financial relations between the two governments.

Initially, it was provided that the imperial contribution should have regard to the relative taxable capacities of Ireland and the United Kingdom, and a sum of £18 million ($43.2 million) was fixed as appropriate. This was, in fact, the sum which Ireland was estimated to be contributing during the financial year in which the problem was examined; Northern Ireland's share was fixed at forty-four per cent or £7,920,000 ($19,008,000). Unfortunately, the provisional estimates of revenue and expenditure proved unduly optimistic, and the idea of a fixed contribution had to be quickly abandoned. The Irish Free State (Consequential Provisions) Act, 1922, restricted the financial provisions in the 1920 Act to Northern Ireland and provided that the initial contribution of £7,920,000 for two years might become 'such less sum as the Joint Exchequer Board may substitute'. A special arbitration committee was set up under Lord Colwyn to consider whether 'in view of the ratification of the Constitution of the Irish Free State, any alteration is needed in the present scale of the Contribution of Northern Ireland to the cost of Imperial Services'.

The committee's first task was to consider the imperial contributions for 1922-3 and 1923-4, and these were fixed at approximately £6.7 million ($16.0 million) and £4.5 million ($10.8 million). In this, the guiding principle was that the contribution should be the surplus of revenue over actual expenditure; a free gift of land purchase annuities was excluded from the calculation of revenue, and provided the new government with additional money not tied to specific purposes. At this stage, Northern Ireland had not diverged significantly from British administrative practice, and its levels of taxation were the same. However, if the imperial contribution was to become a residual figure related mainly to expenditure on the transferred services, it was necessary for the Colwyn Committee to lay down principles by which this expenditure should be determined. These were contained in the committee's final report, published in 1925 :

> The extent to which the total revenue exceeds the actual and necessary expenditure in Northern Ireland shall be taken as the basic sum for determining the contribution, but only after a full consideration by the Joint Exchequer Board of the result of the application of the formula referred to below to the facts of the year under consideration, and so that the contribution shall be such basic sum modified and adjusted as the Joint Exchequer Board may consider just and proper having regard to that result.

In determining the necessary expenditure there shall be eliminated:

(a) all expenditure on any service in existence in both Northern Ireland and Great Britain incurred in providing Northern Ireland with a higher average standard of service than exists in Great Britain;

(b) such expenditure on any service in existence in both Northern Ireland and Great Britain as is incurred in providing an average standard of service, which, while not higher than the average standard of service in Great Britain, is in excess of the strict necessities of the case in Northern Ireland having regard to any lower general level of prices, of wages, or of standards of comfort or social amenity which may exist in Northern Ireland as compared with Great Britain;

(c) all expenditure undertaken by the Government of Northern Ireland on services which do not exist in Great Britain.

From Northern Ireland's point of view, the Colwyn formula was advantageous in making transferred services a first charge on revenue. At the same time, if strictly applied, it could have severely limited the power of the Northern Ireland Parliament to initiate local solutions to local problems. Initially, the financial year 1923-4 was taken as a standard of relative expenditure between Great Britain and Northern Ireland, so that the proper expenditure of future years could be determined. The Colwyn committee advised that the formula might be reconsidered after five years, but in fact it remains as a general guideline. However, there has been no attempt since 1931 to apply the formula in strict mathematical terms. During the 1930s, the imperial contribution fell on occasions to as little as £10,000 ($24,000), and it was apparent that public spending was curtailed for want of revenue. As early as 1925, Sir James Craig had envisaged that a time might come when 'the contribution, instead of being paid by Northern Ireland to Great Britain, may be paid by Great Britain to Northern Ireland in order to preserve the same standard of living amongst the population as prevails on the other side'. In 1932, it was found that to maintain expenditure at the same level as in Great Britain would have entailed a negative contribution of £640,000 ($1,536,000), However, no special payment was made by Great Britain.

A factor in Northern Ireland's financial difficulties was the operation of the Unemployment Insurance Agreement of 1926. From the beginning, the government had committed itself to maintaining parity in cash social services such as unemployment insurance and pensions, although the Colwyn formula allowed for the possibility of something less than this. However, by 1925, heavy unemployment had created a deficit of £3.6 million ($8.6 million) in Northern Ireland's unemployment insurance fund. The British Government recognised the special local problem and referred it to a committee under Lord Cave, which recommended that the British and Northern Ireland funds should be 'reinsured'. The 1926 agreement provided for payments from the Northern Ireland exchequer to reduce any deficit on the local fund to a level equal (per head of insured population) to the deficit on the British fund. The total cost of unemployment to the Northern Ireland exchequer was then determined, and seventy-five per cent of the excess cost (per head of the whole population) as compared with Great Britain was met by the British Government. The system worked moderately well for a few years, and in 1930-1 the payment of £0.54 million ($1.29 million) from the British exchequer was almost identical to the sum paid back as the imperial contribution. This was the last year in which Northern Ireland could pretend to both financial self-sufficiency and British standards of spending.

Two years later, there was no reinsurance payment. Although the cost of unemployment was higher in Northern Ireland, per head of insured population, a significantly smaller proportion of the population were insured. As a result, when the cost was calculated per head of the whole population, it appeared that Northern Ireland was spending less than Great Britain. In consequence, a new agreement was negotiated in 1936. It provided that calculations were in future made solely on the basis of insured population, and the agreement embraced unemployment assistance (introduced in 1934) as well as unemployment insurance. With the eventual easing of the unemployment problem, the last payment under the 1936 agreement was made in 1941-2. One effect of the 1926 and 1936 agreements, of course, was that Northern Ireland was able to avoid a substantial debt which would

L

otherwise have been incurred in making good the deficits in the unemployment insurance fund. By the end of 1946-7, about £23 million ($55 million) had been paid into the fund, of which something over £12 million ($29 million) came from the British exchequer. In Great Britain, by contrast, deficits were met by borrowing.

In 1931, the *Report of the Committee on Financial Relations between the State and Local Authorities* (Cmd 131) concluded that Northern Ireland had reached the limit of its resources. It rejected the idea of any 'serious transference' of the burden of public expenditure to ratepayers, and added : 'We favour the alternative of drastic retrenchment, and we think that, so far as the state is concerned, that path should be pursued even if it leads to the adoption in respect of unemployment benefit and other social services of a level below that which is accepted as the standard for Great Britain'. Retrenchment there was, but there was also substantial pressure from the British Government to find new sources of revenue. The Valuation Acts Amendment Act (NI), 1932, was passed after a threat that the British Government would itself impose a revaluation of Northern Ireland property for income tax purposes. The Finance Act (NI), 1934, included a provision whereby local authorities had to pay the exchequer the product of a 5p (12c) rate as a contribution towards education costs; again, this was done under pressure from London.

However, the 1936 agreement on unemployment insurance indicated that the British Government recognised Northern Ireland's inability to finance services at British levels, and on 12 May 1938 there came a specific guarantee from the Chancellor of the Exchequer, Sir John Simon. In what is known as the Simon declaration, he told the Commons at Westminster that not only should Northern Ireland be entitled to enjoy the same social standards and services as Great Britain, but that if a deficit occurred on its budget which was not the result of a higher standard of expenditure or a lower standard of taxation, means would be found to make good the deficit. This enunciation of the parity principle was welcomed in Northern Ireland, with a warning from the Minister of Finance, Mr J. M. Andrews, that it implied that local authorities must bear the same share of expenditure as their counterparts in Great Britain. An extension of the parity principle was announced on 23 May 1944 by the Minister of Finance, Major J. Maynard Sinclair; he revealed that agreement had been reached with the Chancellor of the Exchequer, Sir John Anderson, providing for Northern Ireland to make up 'leeway' in those services which had lower standards than in Great Britain.

Clearly, 'parity' is difficult to calculate outside the cash social services. Northern Ireland is not a microcosm of the United Kingdom, and it has also chosen to administer some services in quite different ways from Great Britain. Neither government publishes figures indicating how the estimates of spending on the transferred services are arrived at, and the *Ulster Year Book 1950* suggests how flexible the arrangements have become :

> Under earlier arrangements, it rested with the Joint Exchequer Board to determine any question of the admissibility or otherwise of Ulster expenditure, or any other matter arising out of the out-turn of each financial year. The close and harmonious relations which exist between H.M. Treasury and the Ulster Ministry of Finance enable such matters to be settled in advance of submission to the Board. The submission is normally a joint one, and in the light of such agreement the Board seldom institute additional enquiries into the technical details of the joint recommendations. In practice, prior agreement between the two Treasuries is effected under arrangements as follows :—
>
> '(a) Parity of services and taxation between Great Britain and Northern Ireland will be the guiding principle.
>
> (b) The Northern Ireland Budget will be agreed each year between the Treasury and the Ministry of Finance for submission to the Joint Exchequer Board. In submitting Budget proposals for discussion, the Ministry will draw attention to major items of expenditure, and in particular will indicate any proposed divergence from parity standards which is deemed necessary from the aspect of special local conditions.
>
> (c) All Northern Ireland Supplementary Estimates arising in the course of a year will be furnished to the Treasury for their information and agreement as at (b) above.
>
> (d) The Ministry will consult with the Treasury in advance in respect of any new items of Northern Ireland expenditure, other than expenditure incurred on services in parity

with Great Britain, estimated to exceed £50,000
[$120,000] in amount.'

With high taxation and comparatively low levels of
unemployment during World War II, the imperial contribution rose to £36.3 million ($87.1 million) in 1944-5. It
remained a substantial figure for some years, but declined
fairly steadily in the 1950s, and has now become a nominal
figure; the estimate for 1970-1 was £1 million ($2.4 million).
It is apparent that at one period more might have been spent
to make up leeway, and that subsequently the political desire
to have a positive imperial contribution curbed expenditure.
However, it is also true that ways have been found of making
money available to the Northern Ireland exchequer other than
by the attribution of reserved revenue.

In 1946, an interim agreement provided for the reinsurance
of expenditure on unemployment insurance, unemployment
assistance and family allowances. Then, on 5 July 1948, comprehensive schemes of national insurance, national assistance
and health services came into effect throughout the United
Kingdom. The Acts passed in both parliaments provided for
complete financial and administrative reciprocity, and contributions and benefits were the same in both areas. With the
higher level of unemployment in Northern Ireland, payments
in recent years have been in excess of £10 million ($24
million); there have been small counterpayments to Great
Britain's industrial injuries insurance fund. In addition, the
Social Services Agreement of 1949 provided for substantial
reinsurance in national assistance (later called supplementary
benefits), old age and blind persons non-contributory pensions,
temporary unemployment benefit, family allowances and the
health services. This provided that the Northern Ireland
exchequer should bear an amount of the expenditure proportional to its population, and twenty per cent of any excess.
Payments from Great Britain in recent years have been around
£10 million ($24 million), but in 1968-9 exceeded £19 million
($45.6 million).

In agriculture, only the 'remoteness grant' appears in the
Northern Ireland budget; this was fixed at £1.75 million
($4.2 million) per year during 1966-71. Much more important
are the deficiency payments, production grants and other

payments made directly to Northern Ireland farmers and to marketing boards from the United Kingdom exchequer. During the period 1964-9, these averaged almost £27 million ($65 million) per year. Thus, although agriculture is a transferred service under the Government of Ireland Act, 1920, the major part of public spending in this field falls directly on the British budget; less than one-third is attributed to the Ministry of Agriculture at Stormont. In manufacturing industry, the cost of regional employment premiums is met by a special payment from the British exchequer to the Northern Ireland exchequer; in 1969-70, this amounted to £10 million ($24 million).

Northern Ireland has also been able to make minor departures from the principle of parity of taxation. The scope for local initiative in taxation is limited, but there have been variations from British levels of estate duty; these were aimed at easing the problems of family firms, more common in Northern Ireland than in Great Britain. Initially the minister of finance (Major J. Maynard Sinclair in the post-war years) preserved parity by raising a compensating amount of revenue from other taxes; however, his successor (Mr Brian Maginess) made no such gesture when making a further local concession in estate duty in 1954, but the sum involved was small. In recent years, there have been a number of variations from British levels of selective employment tax, as a recognition of Northern Ireland's economic difficulties. Arguably, SET might have been considered to be more properly a reserved tax when it was introduced in 1966, but the decision to collect it through the medium of national insurance meant that it became a transferred tax collected by the Ministry of Health and Social Services. (It also became the major element in transferred tax revenue, almost seventy-two per cent in 1969-70.) The variations have included delaying the introduction of increases in SET, making special 'cushion' payments, and making concessions in some forms of employment. Initially, there was a fifty per cent refund covering male employees in the construction and service industries. In 1968, the minister provided full refunds of SET to hotels outside the Belfast urban area. Arguably, the local variations might more readily have been challenged had they appeared in the context of Finance Acts at Westminster. One tax which was clearly a transferred tax under the 1920 Act was purchase tax, introduced in 1940. However, Northern Ireland could only have claimed the tax actually levied within the region, and would have lost substantially through the collection from wholesalers in Great Britain of tax on goods sold in Northern Ireland. After discussions between the Ministry of Finance and the British Treasury, it was agreed to treat purchase tax as a reserved tax, and a proportion of the total revenue (at first 1.7 per cent, later 2.5 per cent) was attributed to Northern Ireland.

In 1968-9, British payments to Northern Ireland (apart from the residuary share of reserved taxation) amounted to almost £72 million ($172.8 million). Payments to the exchequer totalled £30.4 million, comprising £19.4 million under the Social Services Agreement of 1949, £1.7 million as the agricultural 'remoteness grant', and £9.3 million towards regional employment premiums. There was a payment of £13.3 million into Northern Ireland's national insurance fund. Finally, payments to farmers and marketing boards totalled £28.2 million. Moreover, the imperial contribution of £2 million ($4.8 million) represented a very small part of defence and other national expenditure—and much less than Northern Ireland's 'share' if calculated on a basis of population or even taxable capacity. Under the *Northern Ireland Development Programme 1970-75*, there was a further commitment from the British Government that 'subject to any adjustment which might from time to time be required in connection with the task of managing the economy as a whole, additional finance will be made available where necessary to implement the Programme'. The Northern Ireland Government, for its part, agreed that in 1971 it would withdraw the estate duty concession on the middle range of estates and that in 1972 it would reduce industrial derating from seventy-five per cent to fifty per cent.

The gradual evolution of the Northern Ireland Government's relations with the British Government has reflected the changing financial relations and the increasing measure of financial dependence. In the early years of financial self-sufficiency (and hardship), the Northern Ireland Government

exercised great freedom in those areas where financial consi-
derations were not dominant; in particular, electoral arrangements were manipulated at different levels to benefit unionist
interests. From an early stage, however, the Northern Ireland
Government was also committed to parity in cash social
services, and this ultimately depended on British agreement
to reinsurance arrangements which amounted to subsidisation.
Following the Simon declaration of 1938, and especially
following World War II, the parity principle covered
government spending as a whole. The logical development of
this was that the concept of parity should extend to areas
where finance was not the major consideration. The civil
rights movement in the late 1960s sought essentially to achieve
British standards over a wider area of administration and
policy; Northern Ireland's financial dependence made it
vulnerable to pressure from the British Government or from
public opinion in Great Britain, a vulnerability which was
increased when the civil disorders of August 1969 led to a
dependence on British troops to maintain peace in the streets.

In a broadcast on 9 December 1968, Capt Terence O'Neill
quoted section 75 of the Government of Ireland Act, 1920,
and added :

> Because Westminster has trusted us over the years to use
> the powers of Stormont for the good of all the people of Ulster,
> a sound custom has grown up that Westminster does not use
> its supreme authority in fields where we are normally respon-
> sible. But Mr Wilson [the British prime minister] made it
> absolutely clear to us that if we did not face up to our
> problems the Westminster Parliament might well decide to
> act over our heads.

The point had been made by the Home Secretary, Mr Roy
Jenkins, on 25 October 1967 when he told the British House
of Commons that 'unity can have little meaning unless we
work towards common economic and social standards and
common standards in political tolerance and non-discrimination on both sides of the Irish Sea'. He added that there was
room for argument about the pace which was practicable or
desirable, but 'we must at least be satisfied about the direction.
Provided we can be so satisfied, there is a great deal to be
said for not trying to settle the affairs of Northern Ireland too

directly from London'. Thus, the convention that Westminster should not interfere in matters delegated to Stormont was shown to have limits, though the probability remained that the Northern Ireland Government would yield to pressure rather than force the British Government to ask Westminster to invoke the reserve power contained in section 75. The disturbances of August 1969 brought a new British involvement in Northern Ireland affairs, as was indicated in the joint declaration issued by the two governments following a meeting at Downing Street on 19 August 1969 :

> The United Kingdom Government have ultimate responsibility for the protection of those who live in Northern Ireland when, as in the past week, a breakdown of law and order has occurred. In this spirit, the United Kingdom Government responded to the requests of the Northern Ireland Government for military assistance in Londonderry and Belfast in order to restore law and order. They emphasise again that troops will be withdrawn when law and order has been restored.
>
> The Northern Ireland Government have been informed that troops have been provided on a temporary basis in accordance with the United Kingdom's ultimate responsibility. In the context of the commitment of these troops, the Northern Ireland Government have re-affirmed their intention to take into the fullest account at all times the views of Her Majesty's Government in the United Kingdom, especially in relation to matters affecting the status of citizens of that part of the United Kingdom and their equal rights and protection under the law.

A communique issued after the Downing Street meeting announced that the GOC Northern Ireland (Lieutenant-General Sir Ian Freeland) would immediately assume overall responsibility for security operations, including full command and control of the Ulster Special Constabulary. In addition,

> The United Kingdom Ministers proposed and the Northern Ireland Ministers readily agreed that two senior civil servants from London should be temporarily stationed with the Northern Ireland Government in Belfast to represent the increased concern which the United Kingdom Government had necessarily acquired in Northern Ireland affairs through the commitment of the armed forces in the present conditions.

One civil servant was attached to the prime minister's

department, the other to the Ministry of Home Affairs.

One effect of the disturbances in Northern Ireland and the increasing involvement of the British Government was that it became much easier to discuss Northern Ireland affairs at Westminster; in matters of security and law and order, it was possible to point to a clear ministerial responsibility at Westminster. Secondly, the Northern Ireland Government embarked on an unprecedented series of legislative reforms, following further inter-governmental discussions and the reports of joint working parties. These included the reorganisation of the Royal Ulster Constabulary along the lines of the Hunt report, together with the disbandment of the USC and its replacement by the UDR (part of the British Army) and a small RUC Reserve to assist in normal police duties; a new Ministry of Community Relations and an independent Community Relations Commission; the allocation of public housing on a points system, together with the establishment of a central housing authority; a commissioner for complaints, to investigate allegations of maladministration by local authorities or other public bodies; reform of the local government franchise, and a Local Government Ward Boundaries Commission; measures to ensure fair employment practices in the civil service, local authorities and other public bodies; and the Prevention of Incitement to Hatred Act (NI), 1970.

Under the Community Relations Act (NI), 1969, the new commission was largely an educative and consultative body. Its duty was to 'encourage the establishment of, and assist others to take steps to secure the establishment of, harmonious community relations'. It could also advise any minister (whether by request or not), and was asked to promote the understanding and acceptance of any recommendation made by the commissioner for complaints which appeared to be 'of importance in improving community relations'. Under the Act, the commission has between six and ten members, who include the commissioner for complaints and the parliamentary commissioner for administration. In a communique issued on 29 August 1969—following a visit by the Home Secretary, Mr James Callaghan—the Northern Ireland Government had undertaken that half the members of the commission would be Protestant and half Catholic. The first six nominated members fulfilled this undertaking, but the balance was disturbed by the fact that the ex-officio members were both Protestants; however, a Catholic, Mr Maurice Hayes, was named as chairman. The first commissioner for complaints was Mr J. M. Benn, until then permanent secretary in the Ministry of Education. Unlike the ombudsman, it was possible for complaints to be referred to him directly and not through an MP. In addition to local authorities and new town commissions, he was entitled to investigate such bodies as the Electricity Board for Northern Ireland, the Hospitals Authority and hospital management committees, the General Health Services Board, the Northern Ireland Tourist Board and industrial training boards. The police were outside his competence, as was action taken in the discharge of professional duties of a medical nature. Where the commissioner reports that injustice has been sustained because of maladministration, there is provision for the county court to award compensation and to grant any necessary injunction; the commissioner can also ask the attorney-general to apply to the High Court for an injunction where it appears that the local or public body has engaged in similar maladministration in other cases and may continue to do so.

The Prevention of Incitement to Hatred Act (NI), 1970, was designed to 'deter persons from inciting hatred or fear in the community by threats, abuse or malicious rumours'. Section 1 makes it an offence by the use of threatening, abusive or insulting language to stir up hatred against or arouse fear of any section of the public on the grounds of their religious belief, colour, race or ethnic or national origins. Section 2 covers the publication or circulation of statements or reports known or believed to be false with intent to provoke a breach of the peace and similarly likely to stir up hatred or fear. Two other measures were a response to Northern Ireland's particular problems. The Protection of the Person and Property Act (NI), 1969, was designed to deal with intimidation, which had become common in Belfast, and with the use of petrol bombs. The Criminal Justice (Temporary Provisions) Act (NI), 1970, imposed mandatory minimum prison sentences for a number of offences 'committed during the period of the present emergency'. These offences concerned such matters as explosives, firearms, public order, malicious damage, criminal conspiracy, riot, unlawful assembly, intimidation and carrying offensive weapons; it had the effect of imposing six-month sentences for ordinary 'breach of the peace' offences unrelated to the communal disturbances.

Clearly, relations between Stormont and Westminster changed significantly during the period of continuing disturbances which began with rioting in Londonderry on 5 October 1968. The inter-governmental discussions at Downing Street on 4 November 1968 covered the areas in which the Northern Ireland Government announced reforms on 22 November. On 5 November, Mr Harold Wilson, the British Prime Minister, said at Westminster that if Capt O'Neill or his ideals were overthrown by extremists, the British Government would need to consider a very fundamental reappraisal of its relations with Northern Ireland. Within five months, O'Neill had resigned under pressure from the right wing of his party, but reforms continued under his successor, Major Chichester-Clark. However, the disturbances of August 1969 led to a much more rapid pace of reform than had previously been contemplated, and to reforms which the Northern Ireland Government might never have undertaken in peaceful conditions. The Downing Street declaration of 19 August 1969 imposed some explicit obligations on the Northern Ireland Government in regard to equality of treatment and freedom from discrimination, and in regard to the views of the British Government. Protocol was observed in that subsequent policies and legislative proposals were presented as being decided by the Northern Ireland Government, but it appeared to observers that the government could not have exercised any substantial freedom to dissent from the views of the British Government.

In effect, some important political decisions were taken out of the hands of the Northern Ireland Government by referring them to such bodies as the Hunt committee and the joint working parties; it would have been difficult for the government to turn down their recommendations. A key figure in the political field was the British Government's representative in the prime minister's department; the first appointee was Mr Oliver Wright, a former British ambassador to Denmark, and it was perhaps significant that he came from the Foreign and Commonwealth Office rather than the Home Office. Similarly, while there was a joint security committee on which the government, the police and the army were represented, the dominant figure in security was the director of operations, General Freeland. As to the police, the Inspector-General of the RUC, Mr Anthony Peacocke, resigned when he Hunt report was published; he was succeeded by Sir Arthur Young, Commissioner of the City of London Police. In one sense, a 'very fundamental reappraisal' of relations had taken place under pressure of events; in another sense, it had yet to come, for the British Government found the administration at Stormont willing to accelerate the pace of reform. The unanswered question was what would happen if Stormont set its face against reform, and even tried to reverse some of the measures agreed between the two governments. As Northern Ireland neared the end of fifty years of self-government, it was not certain that a reforming administration could command adequate support from the electorate or from the Unionist Party when opposed by Protestant Unionists and by the right wing of the party. On 10 August 1970, the Home Secretary, Mr Reginald Maudling, gave an explicit warning :

> To go back on what has been done—or depart from the ideal of impartiality and reconciliation—would endanger the present constitutional arrangements under which Northern Ireland governs its own affairs.

7

The Irish Question

The Downing Street declaration of 19 August 1969 began
with firm assurances about Northern Ireland's constitutional
position :

1. The United Kingdom Government re-affirm that nothing
which has happened in recent weeks in Northern Ireland
derogates from the clear pledges made by successive United
Kingdom Governments that Northern Ireland should not
cease to be a part of the United Kingdom without the consent of the people of Northern Ireland or from the provision
in Section 1 of the Ireland Act 1949 that in no event will
Northern Ireland or any part thereof cease to be part of the
United Kingdom without the consent of the Parliament of
Northern Ireland. The Border is not an issue.
2. The United Kingdom Government again affirm that
responsibility for affairs in Northern Ireland is entirely a
matter of domestic jurisdiction. The United Kingdom
Government will take full responsibility for asserting this
principle in all international relationships.

However, the Irish border had been a political issue since its
inception, and the constitutional issue had dominated
northern politics and influenced the use made of the powers
of self-government. On 13 August 1969, the Prime Minister
of the Republic of Ireland, Mr Jack Lynch, disclosed that his
government had asked the British Government to apply
immediately to the United Nations for the urgent despatch of
a peacekeeping force to Northern Ireland. 'Recognising, however, that the reunification of the national territory can provide the only permanent solution for the problem, it is our
intention to request the British Government to enter into
early negotiations with the Irish Government to review the

present constitutional position of the six counties of Northern Ireland.' The British Government remained adamant that Northern Ireland's problems were an internal matter. However, despite the disagreement between the British and Irish governments and the diplomatic offensive mounted from Dublin, Anglo-Irish relations remained cordial; each government was aware of the other's political problems and of the fact that there was no easy solution to the communal violence in Northern Ireland. Nonetheless, the Irish question—so long dormant—threatened to occupy again a prominent position in British political life.

Relations between the governments in Belfast and Dublin had naturally remained strained since the 1920s, and direct contact was somewhat limited by the fact that the northern administration was not a sovereign government. In *Ulster since 1800*, Hugh Shearman wrote :

> Relations between Northern Ireland and the Republic of Ireland have been dominated by the irredentist claims which the Republic has made upon Northern Ireland and by a vigorous propaganda from Dublin. The pre-war constitutional changes in Eire, its wartime neutrality, the establishment of the Republic and the breach with the Commonwealth, have all deepened the gulf between south and north. Several events have shown, however, that between Northern Ireland and the Republic there could be a good deal of the kind of co-operation which the act of 1920 envisaged for the governments of Northern and Southern Ireland. Agreement about the utilization of the River Erne, the administration of the Great Northern Railway and a number of other matters, shows that the two governments can co-operate.

The Erne Drainage and Development Act (NI), 1950, together with corresponding legislation in the Republic, provided for a major drainage scheme in county Fermanagh; in return for contributing to the cost of public works in Northern Ireland, the Republic was able to develop hydro-electricity on the county Donegal section of the River Erne. The Great Northern Railway Board, set up by the two governments, operated from 1953 until 1958, since when separate publicly-owned companies have shared amicably the provision of services on the Belfast-Dublin line. In 1952, the Foyle Fisheries Commission was set up, with two members from each side of the border, and assumed responsibility for protection and conservation in the Foyle drainage area and for the management of fishing rights in Lough Foyle and the tidal portions of the rivers Foyle and Faughan. In such matters, the problem was a localised one posed by the existence of a border; on broader issues, such as the publicising of Ireland as a tourist area, there tended to be little co-operation. One measure indicative of the government's attitude to the Republic was the Safe-guarding of Employment Act (NI), 1947, which introduced a system of employment permits to protect the interests of 'Northern Ireland workers'. A major objective of the Act was to exclude workers from the South, many of whom had taken jobs in Northern Ireland during World War II.

On 14 January 1965, Mr Sean Lemass, Prime Minister of the Republic, crossed the border to have discussions with Capt Terence O'Neill, Prime Minister of Northern Ireland. The discussions were on 'possibilities of practical co-operation in economic matters of mutual interest', and they led to much wider and more open contacts between ministers and civil servants of both governments. Mr Lemass commented: 'Things can never be the same again so far as North-South relations are concerned'. In March 1965, the two governments appointed a joint committee on co-operation in electricity supply, under the chairmanship of Sir Josiah Eccles. A year later, the committee reported that 'The establishment of a substantial connection between the Systems of the Electricity Supply Board [in the Republic] and the Undertakings of Northern Ireland is technically practicable and economically desirable', and an agreement to this effect was signed in October 1967. Closer contacts also developed between the Northern Ireland Tourist Board and its southern counterpart, Bord Failte, and there was some co-operation in promoting Irish holidays.

When the 1965 Anglo-Irish trade treaty came into effect on 1 July 1966, tariffs on most British goods entering the Republic were reduced by ten per cent; for a number of goods manufactured in Northern Ireland, there was a reduction of twenty per cent, and this differential was maintained as succeeding years brought further tariff reductions under the terms of the treaty. However, while the Lemass-O'Neill meeting led to trade talks between the responsible ministers of the two governments, the Republic had earlier shown willingness to give preferential treatment to northern industries; in 1962, significant tariff concessions were granted in respect of linen, paint, electrical motors and furniture. The practical consequences of closer and more harmonious relations between the two governments were more limited than some people had hoped, and the worsening political climate from 1966 onwards prevented inter-governmental contacts from becoming an uncontroversial commonplace. Lemass's successor, Mr Jack Lynch, was in office for more than a year before he met O'Neill at Stormont on 11 December 1967.

The Northern Ireland Government's commitment to the existing constitutional link with Great Britain remained unaltered and apparently inflexible, and O'Neill—who admitted that he had once been attracted to dominion status for Northern Ireland—envisaged similar regional parliaments being set up in Scotland and Wales. However, the civil disorders which began on 5 October 1968 renewed southern interest in the problems of Northern Ireland and caused politicians in the Republic to re-examine their attitudes to partition in an attempt to find a practical solution to 'the Irish question'. Speaking in Tralee on 20 September 1969, Mr Lynch adopted a more conciliatory tone than at the height of the August disturbances :

> . . . in seeking reunification, our aim is not to extend the domination of Dublin. We have many times down the years expressed our willingness to seek a solution on federal lines, and in my most recent statement I envisaged the possibility of intermediate stages in an approach to a final agreed solution. Whatever the constitutional setting might be—and we are prepared to explore all the possibilities in constructive discussion—the united Ireland we desire is one in which there would be a scrupulously fair deal for all. The protestants of the North need have no fear of any interference with their religious freedom or civil liberties and rights. . . . It is unnecessary to repeat that we seek reunification by peaceful means. We are not seeking to overthrow by violence the Stormont parliament or government, but rather to win the agreement of a sufficient number of people in the North to an acceptable form of reunification.

In a subsequent interview, Mr Lynch said that article 44 of

the Republic's constitution was an apparent obstacle to unity, and indicated a willingness to hold a referendum to rescind it. Under section 1 (2) of article 44, 'The State recognises the special position of the Holy Catholic Apostolic and Roman Church as the guardian of the Faith professed by the great majority of the citizens'.

In a reply on 23 September, the Prime Minister of Northern Ireland, Major Chichester-Clark, repeated a number of criticisms of the policies of the Dublin government and of the article in the Republic's constitution asserting sovereignty over all Ireland. However, his tone was equally conciliatory and he set Irish problems in a broader context.

> Mr. Lemass brought into the Government a new realism, which took account of the fact that the destiny of Ireland is inevitably linked with that of her much more powerful and populous neighbour. No really satisfactory and statesman-like view of the future can be formed except in the context of the British Isles as a whole, very probably in increasingly close association with the rest of Europe.
>
> . . . there is no reason . . . why North and South, under two Parliaments, should not wherever possible work together not only for the good of Ireland but for the good of these islands as a whole. . . . All we ask is that our aspirations in Northern Ireland should not be overlooked. Whatever our failings, we represent a bridge between this island and its neighbour.

On 22 October 1969, Mr Lynch told the Dail that his government was studying the possibility of a loose federal or similar arrangement under which Northern Ireland's economic and financial links with Great Britain would be preserved while the Republic pursued its own development policy with an eye to eventual harmonisation. In May 1970, an inter-departmental unit was established in Dublin 'to examine all matters affecting North-South relations; to keep in close touch with all aspects of Anglo-Irish relations having a bearing on the situation; and to arrange for the study in depth of short-term as well as long-term difficulties'. There was a minor diplomatic incident on 6 July 1970 when the Republic's Minister for External Affairs, Dr Patrick Hillery, visited secretly the Catholic Falls Road area of Belfast following disturbances there. This was described by the

M

British Foreign Secretary, Sir Alec Douglas-Home, as a 'serious diplomatic discourtesy', in that the British Government had not been consulted in advance, but relations between the governments in Dublin and London were not seriously impaired. On 11 July 1970, Mr Lynch addressed the British Government and people in a broadcast, saying :

> Why should we, the Celts and the English, go on misunderstanding each other? There is no imperial role for you in Ireland. We have fought the good fight against each other. Neither of us should claim victory, because that is never the best result. Is it not better that we should both claim, as civilised peoples, the capacity to settle the last remaining disagreement between us by peaceful means?

To the northern Protestants, he posed the question : 'Do you mistrust yourselves so much as to refuse to see that your home is here—not across any waters?'

For the Northern Ireland Government, there was no question of reopening the 1921 settlement, and Major Chichester-Clark made it clear that he would be unwilling to engage in tripartite talks with the British and Irish governments. Nor was there any evidence that northern Protestants as a whole were ready to respond to overtures from the Republic. However, the conciliatory character of Mr Lynch's broadcast—in which he spoke of 'your own great tradition'—contrasted with signs of growing British impatience at Northern Ireland's failure to solve its problems. Peace in Northern Ireland depended very much on the presence of British troops, a graphic commentary on the progress of the fifty-year-old experiment in devolution.

8

Success or Failure?

It could not be said, as Northern Ireland struggled uneasily through its fiftieth year of self-government, that the experiment in devolution had manifestly succeeded. At best, it might be argued that it had proved (most of the time, at least) a workable solution to a desperately difficult problem, and that all or most other solutions might have proved less workable. It is a hypothetical argument, though, and it is perhaps pointless to consider whether the problems of Protestant-Catholic relations would have been better dealt with in a Westminster context or whether northern unionists would have come to terms with a united Ireland and lived amicably with their Catholic neighbours.

Some conclusions can be drawn which are relevant to the possible establishment of other regional administrations in the United Kingdom; some aspects of the Northern Ireland situation have no relevance to other regions. The fact that devolution was not sought by any substantial section of the Northern Ireland population was an unpromising portent; the Unionists who assumed power in 1921 had no particular commitment to make devolution work for the benefit of the whole community. Devolution as envisaged in the Government of Ireland Act, 1920, never came into effect; the Council of Ireland never functioned. Northern Ireland was from the beginning in the unusual position that its existence as part of the United Kingdom was under constant challenge, whether by peaceful or other methods, whether internally or externally. This influenced and possibly dictated some of the character of government, just as it has influenced the course of party politics. Similarly, there has been no fundamental appraisal of the working of the 1920 Act, simply because the government has felt on the defensive and consequently has been unwilling to reopen constitutional issues. Some changes of a technical nature have been made, and ways have been found to bypass the original intentions of the 1920 Act, but parliamentary scrutiny of the workings of devolution has been minimal. Presumably this could not continue if there were a number of regional administrations seeking to draw on the British exchequer.

The financial provisions of devolution in Northern Ireland are obviously unsatisfactory, however generously the area is treated. Northern Ireland's freedom to administer the transferred services is severely circumscribed by the Treasury's financial control, and at times the separation of local revenue (including the reserved taxes) from the national accounts has curbed necessary expenditure. Neither parliament exercises real oversight of the negotiations which lead each year to the Northern Ireland budget, and Stormont has not been able to exercise any significant independence in imposing local taxes. Presumably, if there were a number of regional administrations drawing on central resources, there would have to be provision for a degree of oversight acceptable to Westminster MPs. Presumably, too, a deliberate effort might be made to finance an appreciable proportion of local expenditure through taxes (for example, sales taxes) which could be levied and varied locally.

Northern Ireland's independence in transferred services is also circumscribed by the power reserved to Westminster in section 75 of the 1920 Act. Arguably, recent events have shown that this power—or the threat that it might be invoked—is necessary in respect of Stormont, and might be desirable in respect of any other regional administrations. Increasingly, the price of parity in the transferred services is not merely parity of taxation but also a willingness to observe or impose accepted British standards in a number of areas of administration and social policy. So far, these areas have largely been ones in which Protestant-Catholic relations are intimately involved. Much of the evidence to the Commission on the Constitution has been concerned with such problems. One solution would be to place within Westminster's competence all legislation on matters of human rights; another would be to amend the 1920 Act, so as to include more effective guarantees of human rights. So far, there has not been real pressure on Stormont to adopt recent British reforms in such matters as homosexuality, abortion, divorce and capital punishment; Northern Ireland has been free to work out its own policies on issues as varied as comprehensive education, liquor-licensing laws, road traffic and penal law. Inevitably, though, public and professional opinion tends to move in much the same direction as opinion in Great Britain but usually with some time-lag. A good deal of social legislation is directly modelled on Westminster Acts.

The fact that one party has held power since 1921 has not been conducive to the development of effective parliamentary debate. There has not been the same incentive towards a consensus of views, as there is at Westminster, where power is expected to change hands at intervals. The opposition has had little function in law-making; while the government has lately proved more willing to take account of opposition arguments, many opponents of the Unionist Party still consider extra-parliamentary activity more likely to get results. Obviously the nature of one-party government has reflected the particular local problems, but other regional parliaments could suffer to a lesser degree by finding that one party continually held power.

The administration at Stormont—both ministers and civil servants—is generally conceded to be a very accessible one, though even in the small area of Northern Ireland there are critics who complain that it favours the Belfast region at the expense of the western counties. Safeguards against maladministration have recently been introduced, and it could be argued that Stormont's best role would be as an administrative rather than a legislative body, or possibly that the legislature should be concerned with the means of implementing national policies in a local situation. With the increasing involvement of the British Government in transferred matters, Stormont has in effect moved into this sort of position. While the Northern Ireland Government insists that it retains freedom of action within the terms of the Downing Street declaration of 19 August 1969, this may seem to outsiders as merely the freedom to decide to do what the British Government wants; it is not clear that the Northern Ireland Government could choose on a major issue to follow a policy that was in direct conflict with British wishes. This relationship could well be put on a more formal basis, with the local legislature and administration acting in effect as agents of Westminster, exercising a defined degree of discretion and subject to an oversight which ensured that the discretion was not abused. While this might seem to diminish Stormont's powers, it would in a real sense increase them by defining them, and the individual MP might find he had a greater opportunity to influence local decisions. The 1920 Act provided for a division of powers and responsibilities which has proved unsatisfactory in different ways, and whose sharp lines have become blurred in practice. This does not mean that the division could not be redrawn.

Bibliography

Barritt, Denis P. and Carter, Charles F. *The Northern Ireland Problem: A Study in Group Relations* (1962)

Beckett, J. C. *A Short History of Ireland* (1952)

Beckett, J. C. *The Making of Modern Ireland 1603-1923* (1966)

Beckett, J. C. and Glasscock, R. E. (eds). *Belfast: The Origin and Growth of an Industrial City* (1967)

Boyd, Andrew. *Holy War in Belfast* (1969)

Calvert, Harry. *Constitutional Law in Northern Ireland: A Study in Regional Government* (1968)

Campbell, J. J. *Catholic Schools: A Survey of a Northern Ireland Problem* (Belfast 1964)

Coogan, Timothy Patrick. *Ireland since the Rising* (1966)

Coogan, Timothy Patrick. *The I.R.A.* (1970)

Corkey, William. *Episode in the History of Protestant Ulster 1923-1947* (Belfast 1960)

Curtis, Edmund. *A History of Ireland* (1936)

de Paor, Liam. *Divided Ulster* (1970)

Dewar, M. W. *Why Orangeism?* (Belfast 1959)

Dewar, M. W., Brown, John and Long, S. E. *Orangeism: A New Historical Appreciation* (Belfast 1967)

Edwards, Owen Dudley. *The Sins of Our Fathers: Roots of Conflict in Northern Ireland* (1970)

Ervine, St John. *Craigavon, Ulsterman* (1949)

Evans, E. Estyn. *Irish Heritage: The Landscape, the People and Their Work* (Dundalk 1942)

Evans, E. Estyn. *Irish Folk Ways* (1957)

Evans, E. Estyn. *Prehistoric and Early Christian Ireland: A Guide* (1966)

Freeman, T. W. *Ireland: A General and Regional Geography* (3rd edn, 1965)

Hurley, Michael (ed). *Irish Anglicanism 1869-1969* (Dublin 1970)

Jones, Emrys (ed). *Belfast in its Regional Setting: A Scientific Survey* (Belfast 1952)

Jones, Emrys. *A Social Geography of Belfast* (1960)

Lawrence, R. J. *The Government of Northern Ireland: Public Finance and Public Services 1921-1964* (1965)

Macalister, R. A. S. *The Archaeology of Ireland* (2nd edn,1949)

Macardle, Dorothy. *The Irish Republic* (4th edn, Dublin 1951)

MacManus, Francis (ed). *The Years of the Great Test 1926-39* (Cork 1967)

Mansergh, Nicholas. *The Government of Northern Ireland: A Study in Devolution* (1936)

Mansergh, Nicholas. *The Irish Question 1840-1921* (1965)

McNeill, Ronald. *Ulster's Stand for Union* (1922)

Mogey, John M. *Rural Life in Northern Ireland* (1947)

Moody, T. W. and Beckett, J. C. (eds). *Ulster Since 1800: A Political and Economic Survey* (1954)

Moody, T. W. and Beckett, J. C. (eds). *Ulster Since 1800: A Social Survey* (1957)

Moody, T. W. and Martin, F. X. (eds). *The Course of Irish History* (Cork 1967)

Neill, Desmond G. (ed). *Devolution of Government: The Experiment in Northern Ireland* (1953)

Nowlan, Kevin B. and Williams, T. Desmond (eds). *Ireland in the War Years and After 1939-51* (Dublin 1969)

O'Neill, Terence. *Ulster at the Crossroads* (1969)

Report of the Irish Boundary Commission 1925 (Shannon 1969)

Riddell, Patrick. *Fire over Ulster* (1970)

Rhodes, Edwin (ed). *Public Administration in Northern Ireland* (Londonderry 1967)

Shearman, Hugh. *Not an Inch: A Study of Northern Ireland and Lord Craigavon* (1942)

Sheehy, Michael. *Divided We Stand: A Study of Partition* (1955)

Stewart, A. T. Q. *The Ulster Crisis* (1967)

Wallace, Martin. *Drums and Guns: Revolution in Ulster* (1970)

Williams, Desmond (ed). *The Irish Struggle 1916-1926* (1966)

Wilson, Thomas (ed). *Ulster Under Home Rule: A Study of the Political and Economic Problems of Northern Ireland* (1955)

Government publications

Queckett, A. S. *The Constitution of Northern Ireland,* parts 1-3 (1928, 1933 and 1946)

The Constitution of Northern Ireland, being the Government of Ireland Act 1920 as amended to 31st December 1968 (1969)

Commission on the Constitution: Written Evidence 3: The Home Office (Note on the Status of Northern Ireland within the United Kingdom); Government Departments of Northern Ireland (1969)

First Report of the Northern Ireland Special Arbitration Committee (United Kingdom command paper 2072, 1924); report of the Colwyn committee

Final Report of the Northern Ireland Special Arbitration Committee (UK Cmd 2389, 1925); report of the Colwyn committee

Financial Statement of Revenue and Expenditure (annual Northern Ireland budget statement)

Financial Accounts (annual)

Reports of the Public Accounts Committee (annual)

Report of the Committee on Financial Relations between the State and Local Authorities (Cmd 131, 1931)

Report of the Committee on the Finances of Local Authorities (Cmd 369, 1957); the Nugent report

The Re-Shaping of Local Government: Statement of Aims (Cmd 517, 1967)

The Re-Shaping of Local Government: Further Proposals (Cmd 530, 1969)

Report of the Review Body on Local Government in Northern Ireland (Cmd 546, 1970); the Macrory report

Local Authority Financial Returns (annual)

Local Authority Rate Statistics (annual)

Interim Report of the Departmental Committee on the

Educational Services in Northern Ireland (Cmd 6, 1922); report of the Lynn committee

Final Report of the Departmental Committee on the Educational Services in Northern Ireland (Cmd 15, 1923); report of the Lynn committee

Educational Reconstruction in Northern Ireland (Cmd 226, 1944)

Educational Development in Northern Ireland (Cmd 470, 1964)

Higher Education in Northern Ireland (Cmd 475, 1965); the Lockwood report

Higher Education in Northern Ireland: Government Statement (Cmd 480, 1965)

Local Education Authorities and Voluntary Schools (Cmd 513, 1967)

Public Education in Northern Ireland (1970)

Report of the Committee on the Health Services in Northern Ireland (Cmd 334, 1955)

The Administrative Structure of the Health and Personal Social Services in Northern Ireland (1969)

Location of Industry in Northern Ireland: Interim Report of the Planning Advisory Board (Cmd 225, 1944)

Planning Proposals for the Belfast Area: Interim Report of the Planning Commission (Cmd 227, 1945)

The Ulster Countryside: Interim Report of the Northern Ireland Planning Advisory Board (1947)

Planning Proposals for the Belfast Area: Second Report of the Planning Commission (Cmd 302, 1952)

Isles, K. S. and Cuthbert, Norman. *An Economic Survey of Northern Ireland* (1957); the Isles report

Report of the Joint Working Party on the Economy of Northern Ireland (Cmd 446, 1962); the Hall report

Belfast Regional Survey and Plan: Recommendations and Conclusions (Cmd 451, 1963); the Matthew plan

Belfast Regional Survey and Plan (1964); the full Matthew plan

The Administration of Town and Country Planning in Northern Ireland (Cmd 465, 1964)

Economic Development in Northern Ireland (Cmd 479, 1965); the Wilson plan

Northern Ireland Development Programme 1970-75 (1970)
Northern Ireland Development Programme 1970-75: Government Statement (Cmd 547, 1970)
Manpower: An Appraisal of the Position 1964-1970 (Northern Ireland Economic Council, 1967)
Area Development in Northern Ireland (Northern Ireland Economic Council, 1969)
Northern Ireland Economic Report (annual)
Northern Ireland Railways (Cmd 458, 1963); the Benson report
Electricity in Ireland: Report of the Joint Committee on Co-operation in Electricity Supply (1966)
Disturbances in Northern Ireland (Cmd 532, 1969); the Cameron report
A Commentary by the Government of Northern Ireland to Accompany the Cameron Report (Cmd 534, 1969)
Report of the Advisory Committee on Police in Northern Ireland (Cmd 535, 1969); the Hunt report
Formation of The Ulster Defence Regiment (UK Cmd 4188, 1969)
Royal Ulster Constabulary Reserve (Cmd 536, 1969)
Ulster Year Book (Originally triennial, now annual)
Digest of Statistics (biannual)
Apart from the United Kingdom papers indicated above, all the foregoing government publications are published in Belfast by Her Majesty's Stationery Office.

Newspapers

Belfast Telegraph
The Irish News, Belfast
News Letter, Belfast
Irish Independent, Dublin
The Irish Press, Dublin
The Irish Times, Dublin

Index